IELTS®

2009–2010 Edition

KAPLAN
PUBLISHING
New York

IELTS® is a registered trademark of University of Cambridge ESOL Examinations, British Council and IDP Education Australia, which neither sponsor nor endorse this product.

This publication is designed to provide accurate and authoritative information in regard to the subject matter covered. It is sold with the understanding that the publisher is not engaged in rendering legal, accounting, or other profes¬sional service. If legal advice or other expert assistance is required, the services of a competent professional should be sought.

© 2009 Kaplan, Inc.

Published by Kaplan Publishing, a division of Kaplan, Inc.

1 Liberty Plaza, 24th Floor

New York, NY 10006

Printed in the United States of America

10 9 8 7 6 5 4 3

ISBN: 978-1-4277-9961-6

Kaplan Publishing books are available at special quantity discounts to use for sales promotions, employee premiums, or educational purposes. Please email our Special Sales Department to order or for more information at kaplanpublishing@kaplan.com, or write to Kaplan Publishing, 1 Liberty Plaza, 24th Floor, New York, NY 10006.

CONTENTS

PART 1: THE BASICS

PART 2: STRATEGIES AND PRACTICE

Chapter 5: The Speaking Module 167

PART 3: PRACTICE TESTS

PART 4: AUDIO TRANSCRIPTS

KAPLAN

IELTS

PART 1:

THE BASICS

CHAPTER 1: WHAT IS THE IELTS?

IELTS stands for International English Language Testing System. It is taken by people who are required to certify their level of English proficiency for educational, vocational and immigration purposes, and measures a person's ability to communicate in English across four language skills—listening, reading, writing and speaking.

WHO ADMINISTERS THE IELTS?

IELTS is developed and delivered through the partnership of the University of Cambridge ESOL Examinations, British Council and IDP Education Australia. It is currently administered at over 300 centres operating in more than 100 countries. Centres supervise the local administration of the test and recruit, train and monitor IELTS examiners.

IELTS sessions are administered according to local needs. Most centres conduct a testing session at least once a month. Test results are available within two weeks. You will receive only one copy of your results, but additional copies of the Test Report Form may be sent to organisations specified by you.

There are no restrictions on retaking the test. However, if you want to retake the test immediately after receiving your first results, you may need to wait, due to the time needed to complete the registration process.

WHO TAKES THE IELTS?

The Academic IELTS is taken by people who wish to enrol in undergraduate and postgraduate courses, and those who wish to undertake work experience at a graduate and post-graduate level.

The General Training IELTS is taken by people who are going to English-speaking countries to complete their secondary education or undertake work experience or training programmes, or by people who are planning to immigrate to Australia, Canada and New Zealand.

LANGUAGE USED ON THE IELTS

The IELTS test is a British test created by UCLES (University of Cambridge Local Examination Syndicate) in the UK. It is written in British English.

Since the IELTS is an international test, the vocabulary and syntax used will be completely understandable to anyone who has studied English in an English-speaking country. If you don't recognize a word at first, you will be able to assess the meaning of the word through its context in the sentence. In addition, you do not have to use British English in the writing module. However, you must use just one form of English consistently—that is, either British or American when writing the exam.

The main differences between British and American English are in spelling and word usage. Here are some examples:

Suffixes	
American English	British English
-am (program)	-amme (programme)
-k (check, bank)	-que (cheque, banque)
-er (center, theater)	-re (centre, theatre)
-ize (apologize, organize)	-ise (apologise, organise)
-or (color, honor, flavor)	-our (colour, honour, flavour)
-og (dialog, catalog)	-ogue (dialogue, catalogue)
-yze (analyze, paralyze)	-yse (analyse, paralyse)

Double / Single Consonants	
American English	British English
appall	appal
enroll	enrol
fulfill, fulfillment	fulfil, fulfilment
skillful	skilful
willful	wilful
jewelry	jewellery
counselor	counsellor
modeling	modelling
traveler	traveller

Word Usage	
American English	British English
gasoline	petrol
major	subject
truck	lorry
pants	trousers
mail a letter	post a letter
faculty	staff
trash	rubbish
vacation	holiday
store	shop
restroom	loo
flashlight	torch

DIFFERENCES BETWEEN THE ACADEMIC AND THE GENERAL TRAINING TESTS

All candidates take the same Listening and Speaking tests. However, there is a choice between Academic and General Training in the Reading and Writing tests.

GENERAL TRAINING READING TEST

The texts are based on the type of material you would be expected to encounter on a daily basis in an English-speaking country. They come from newspapers, notices, official documents, booklets, leaflets, timetables, advertisements, instruction manuals and books, and test your ability to understand and use information.

The first section contains texts relevant to basic linguistic survival in English with tasks that mainly require ability to retrieve and provide general factual information. The second section focuses on the training context—for example, the training programme itself or students' welfare needs. The third section involves reading a longer descriptive text with a more complex structure.

ACADEMIC READING TEST

There are three reading passages with tasks. Texts are taken from books, magazines, journals and newspapers, all written for a non-specialist audience. They may contain visual materials such as diagrams, graphs or illustrations, and deal with issues that are appropriate and accessible to candidates entering undergraduate or postgraduate courses. At least one text contains a detailed logical argument.

GENERAL TRAINING WRITING TEST

The first task requires you to write a letter of at least 150 words either asking for information, or explaining a situation. For the second task, you need to write a short essay of at least 250 words in response to a statement or question on a given topic of general interest. You are expected to demonstrate your ability to:

- discuss issues
- provide general factual information
- describe a problem and present a solution
- present and possibly justify an opinion, assessment or hypothesis
- present and possibly evaluate and challenge ideas, evidence and arguments

ACADEMIC WRITING TEST

The first task requires you to write a description of at least 150 words. This is based on material found in a chart, table, graph or diagram, and demonstrates your ability to:

- present information
- summarise the main features of the input

For the second task, you are required to write a short essay of at least 250 words in response to an opinion or question. The issues raised are suitable for and easily understood by candidates entering undergraduate or postgraduate studies. You are expected to demonstrate your ability to:

- discuss abstract issues
- present a solution to a problem
- present and justify an opinion
- compare and contrast evidence, opinions and implications
- evaluate and challenge ideas, evidence or an argument

HOW THE IELTS IS STRUCTURED

IELTS is divided in two parts: written and oral. The written part consists of Listening, Reading and Writing tests and must be completed on the same day. There is no break between the tests. The oral part of the test may be taken within the period of seven days before or after the written part.

Listening Module Task Types

- Note/summary/flow-chart/table completion
- Multiple choice
- Short-answer questions
- Sentence completion
- Labelling a diagram
- Classification
- Matching

Reading Module Task Types

- Multiple choice
- Short-answer questions
- Sentence completion
- Note/summary/flow-chart/table completion
- Labelling a diagram
- Choosing headings for paragraphs/sections of a text
- Locating information
- Identification of information in the text
- Identification of writer's views/claims
- Classification
- Matching lists/phrases
- Multiple matching

Writing Module Task Types

- Academic Writing
  - Task 1, you are given visual information (graph/table/chart/diagram)
  - In Task 2, you are presented with a point of view, an argument or a problem.
- General Training
  - In Task 1, you must write a letter requesting information or explaining a situation.
  - In Task 2, you are presented with a point of view, argument or problem.

Speaking Module Task Types

- Part 1: Introduction and Interview
- Part 2: Individual Long Turn
- Part 3: Two-way Discussion

LISTENING TEST

The Listening test takes around 30 minutes. There are 40 questions and four sections. During the test, you are given time to read the questions, write down your answers and then check them. The audio for the Listening test is played only once. You should write your answers on the question paper as you listen. When the recording ends, ten minutes are allowed for you to transfer your answers to an answer sheet.

Task Types

The first two sections are concerned with social needs. There is a conversation between two speakers in the first section. For example, it could be a conversation between two people organising an event and discussing their options regarding venues and food available. The second section contains a monologue, which could, for example, be a speech about student services on a university campus or arrangements for meals during an event.

The final two sections are concerned with situations related more closely to educational or training contexts. In the third section, there is a conversation among up to four people. It could be a talk among three students discussing a research project. The fourth section contains another monologue, which could be a lecture or talk of general academic interest.

A range of native-speaker English accents are used in the test. A variety of questions are used, selected from the following types:

- Note/summary/flow-chart/table completion
- Multiple choice
- Short-answer questions
- Sentence completion
- Labelling a diagram
- Classification
- Matching

TASK TYPE 1: OUTLINE COMPLETION

You have to fill in gaps in an outline that covers part or all of the listening text. In order to complete the task, you may have to choose your answers from a list on the question paper or identify the missing words from the recording that fit into the outline. You should not change the words from the recording in any way, and should keep to the word limit stated in the instructions.

The text could be a form, a set of notes, a table, a flow chart or a summary. The answers will focus on the main ideas in the text. In all cases except the summary, notation form can be used to complete the gaps, which means that articles and auxiliary verbs may be omitted when they are not necessary for the meaning. The summary consists of connected sentences and must therefore be grammatically correct.

TASK TYPE 2: MULTIPLE CHOICE

Multiple choice items may include a question followed by three possible answers. You have to choose the one correct answer: **A**, **B** or **C**. They may require you to understand specific points or the main points of the listening text.

The task may also involve sentence completion. You will be given the first part of a sentence and will have to choose the best way to complete it from the options given. Sometimes you are given a longer list of possible answers, and told that you have to choose more than one of them.

TASK TYPE 3: SHORT-ANSWER QUESTIONS

You have to write an answer to a question using information from the recording. You should read the instructions carefully, as they indicate the word limit given for each task. Sometimes you are given a question that asks you to list two or three points.

TASK TYPE 4: SENTENCE COMPLETION

You need to read a set of sentences summarising key information from the entire listening text or from one part of it. You have to complete a gap in each sentence using information from the listening text. You usually have to write no more than three words and/or a number. The words will be taken directly from the listening text and written in the space on your question paper, to be transferred later.

TASK TYPE 5: LABELLING A DIAGRAM, PLAN OR MAP

You have to complete labels on a visual such as a diagram, set of pictures, plan of a building or a map of a part of a town. The answers are usually selected from a list on the question paper.

Task Type 6: Classification

You have to match a numbered list of items from the listening text to a set of criteria. This task type is designed to test your ability to recognize relationships and connections between facts in the listening text. It is therefore often used with texts dealing with factual information. This task tests your ability to listen for detail.

Task Type 7: Matching

You have to match a numbered list of items from the listening text to a set of items in a box. Many variations of this task type are possible regarding the types of options to be matched.

READING TEST

The Reading test takes 60 minutes. There are 40 questions, based on three reading passages containing a total of 2,000 to 2,750 words. Texts and questions appear on a question paper that you can write on but cannot remove from the examination room. All answers must be entered on an answer sheet during the 60-minute test. No extra time is allowed for transferring answers.

Task Types

A variety of questions are used, chosen from the following types:

- Multiple choice

- Short-answer questions

- Sentence completion

- Note/summary/flow-chart/table completion

- Labelling a diagram

- Choosing headings for paragraphs/sections of a text

- Locating information

- Identification of information in the text—True, False or Not Given / Identification of writer's views/claims—Yes, No or Not Given

- Classification

- Matching lists/phrases

- Multiple matching

TASK TYPE 1: MULTIPLE CHOICE

Multiple choice questions are used to test a wide range of reading skills. Some of these questions, for example, may require you to understand specific points or the main points of the text. You are required to select the best answer from several options (for example, **A**, **B**, **C** or **D**), and to write the letter of the answer you have chosen on the answer sheet. The questions are given in the same order as the information in the passage.

TASK TYPE 2: SHORT-ANSWER QUESTIONS

Short-answer questions require you to read the passage for detail; these questions test your ability to find and understand precise, usually factual, information. In general, these questions follow the order in which the information is given in the passage.

You are required to write your answers in words or numbers on the answer sheet. You should read the instructions carefully, as they state the number of words and/or numbers that you are required to write. Numbers can be given in figures or words. Hyphenated words count as single words.

Contracted words will not be tested. If you write more than the number of words asked for, you will lose the mark even if your answer includes the correct word.

Task Type 3: Sentence Completion

There are two variations of this task. The first requires you to complete the sentence in a given number of words taken from the passage. The maximum number of words that can be used is given in the instructions. Numbers can be written as figures or words. The words should be taken directly from the passage, and written in the appropriate spaces on the answer sheet. If you write more than the number of words asked for, you will lose the mark even if your answer includes the correct word.

The second variation requires you to choose the best option from a list. There will be more options to choose from than there are questions. In this task, you should write the letter of your choice on the answer sheet.

Task Type 4: Note/Summary/Flow-Chart/Table Completion

This task type typically relates to precise factual information, and is therefore often used with descriptive passages. There are two variations of this task. The first requires you to select words and/or numbers from the passage. You are given a summary of a section of the passage, and are required to complete it with information taken from the passage. The summary will usually cover only one part of the passage rather than the whole text. The given information may be in the form of a summary, a table with empty cells, several connected notes or a flow chart with missing elements. The answers will also come from one passage section rather than from the entire passage. The second variation requires you to select answers from a list of answers, which often consist of a single word.

Task Type 5: Labelling a Diagram That Has Numbered Parts

This task type is often used with texts describing processes or with descriptive texts. You are required to label numbered parts of a diagram that relates to a description contained in the passage. You will write the correct labels in the spaces on your answer sheet. These labels may consist of up to three words, and be a combination of words, and numbers taken directly from the passage. This will be clearly indicated in the instructions. The answer will usually come from one passage section rather than from the entire passage.

Task Type 6: Choosing Headings for Paragraphs or Sections of a Text

This task type is used with passages that contain paragraphs or sections with clearly defined themes. You are given a list of headings that are usually identified with lower-case Roman numerals (for example, i, ii, iii). Each heading will refer to the main idea of a paragraph or section, and you must match the heading with alphabetically marked paragraphs or sections of the text. You are required to write the appropriate Roman numerals in the spaces on your answer sheet. There will always be more headings than there are paragraphs or sections, so that some headings will not be used. Some paragraphs or sections may not be included in the task. One or more paragraphs or sections may already be matched with a heading as an example.

TASK TYPE 7: LOCATING INFORMATION

This task type may test a wide range of reading skills, from locating detail to recognising a summary or definition. You are asked to find specific information (for example, reasons for an event, descriptions, comparisons, summaries, or explanations) in the numbered paragraphs of the passage, and to write the letters corresponding to the correct paragraph in the spaces on your answer sheet. There may be more than one piece of information that you need to find in a given paragraph. In such cases, you will be told that you can use a letter more than once.

TASK TYPE 8: IDENTIFICATION OF WRITER'S VIEWS/CLAIMS OR OF INFORMATION IN A TEXT

This task type has two variations:

1. Do the following statements agree with the views/claims of the writer? This variation is designed to test your ability to recognise opinions or ideas and is therefore usually used with discursive or argumentative texts. You are required to write 'Yes', 'No' or 'Not Given' in the spaces on your answer sheet.

2. Do the following statements agree with the information in the text? This variation tests your ability to identify specific points of information given in the text. Consequently, it is often used with factual texts. You are asked to write 'True', 'False' or 'Not Given' in the spaces on your answer sheet.

TASK TYPE 9: CLASSIFICATION

This task type is designed to test your ability to recognise relationships and connections between facts in the passage, and is most often used with texts dealing with factual information. You need to be able to scan the passage to locate the required information, and to read for detail.

You are asked to classify events, characteristics or other pieces of information in the passage into given categories. For example, you might be asked to classify developments in rocket technology according to the country where they took place.

Categories are identified by letters, and you are asked to write the correct letter in the corresponding space on your answer sheet. There will normally be a larger number of events or characteristics than there are groups into which to classify them, so a number of questions may be answered with the same letter.

TASK TYPE 10: MATCHING

This task type is designed to test your ability to recognise opinions or theories. You are given a number of options (for example, names of people) and are required to match them with a theory, discovery or statement credited to them. You will write the letters of the correct options in the boxes on your answer sheet. It is possible that some options may never be used and that others may be used more than once. The instructions will indicate whether an option may be used more than once.

TASK TYPE 11: MULTIPLE MATCHING

In this task type, you are given a number of options, and you must match the options provided in the items to extracts or to paragraphs or sections of the passage. The extracts, sections or paragraphs are identified by letter. It is possible that some options may never be used and that others may be used more than once. The instructions will indicate whether an option may be used more than once. This task type is designed to test your ability to skim and scan to identify specific information.

WRITING TEST

 The Writing test takes 60 minutes. There are two tasks to complete. You are advised to spend about 20 minutes on Task 1 and write at least 150 words. Task 2 requires at least 250 words and should take approximately 40 minutes.

You may write on the question paper, but this may not be taken from the examination room and will not be seen by the examiner. Answers must be given on the answer sheet and must be written in full. Notes or bullet points are not acceptable as answers.

Task Types: Academic Writing

In Task 1, you are asked to describe some given visual information (graph/table/chart/diagram) in your own words. Depending on the type of visual input and the specific task given, you are assessed on your ability to organise, present and compare data; describe the stages of a process or procedure; describe an object or event or sequence of events; or explain how something works.

In Task 2, you are presented with a point of view, an argument or a problem. You are assessed on your ability to present the solution to a problem; present and justify an opinion; compare and contrast evidence, opinions and implications; or evaluate and challenge ideas, evidence or an argument.

The issues raised are suitable for and understood by candidates entering undergraduate or postgraduate studies.

Task Types: General Training Writing

In Task 1, you are asked to respond to a given problem with a letter requesting information or explaining a situation. Depending on the specific task given, you are assessed on your ability to engage in personal correspondence; elicit and provide general factual information; express needs, wants, likes and dislikes; or express opinions, views or complaints.

In Task 2, you are presented with a point of view, argument or problem. You are assessed on your ability to provide general factual information; outline a problem and present a solution; present and justify an opinion, assessment or hypothesis; or present and possibly evaluate and challenge ideas, evidence or an argument.

The topics are of general interest and do not require any specialist knowledge on your part.

SPEAKING TEST

The Speaking test consists of a three-part oral interview between you and an examiner and takes between 11 and 14 minutes. All speaking tests are recorded.

Part 1: Introduction and Interview

The examiner introduces him/herself and verifies your identity (you must have a valid ID or passport). The examiner asks you questions from up to three familiar topics. The first topic, for example, may be about your work or studies. The second could be about activities that you like doing in your free time. The third topic could deal with your views on public transport in the area where you live. This task lasts roughly 4–5 minutes.

Part 2: Individual Long Turn

You are given a task card with a topic and list of items that you must discuss during this task. There will be one minute allotted for preparation and making notes; you then talk for about two minutes. If you do not finish within two minutes, the examiner will stop you. The examiner will ask one or two questions to round off the long turn. This section takes roughly 3–4 minutes, including the one-minute preparation time.

Part 3: Two-way Discussion

The examiner invites you to participate in discussion based on questions linked to Part 2.

Speech Functions Often Used by Candidates

During the speaking test, you will usually use the following speech functions:

- Analysing
- Comparing
- Contrasting
- Conversation repair
- Explaining
- Expressing a preference
- Expressing opinions
- Justifying opinions
- Narrating and paraphrasing

- Providing non-personal information
- Providing personal information
- Speculating
- Suggesting
- Summarising

Other speech functions may be used during the test, but they are not obliged by the test structure.

HOW THE IELTS IS SCORED

Correct answers in each of the IELTS tests are translated into a score on the IELTS nine-band scale. Test takers get separate band scores for each of the Reading, Writing, Listening and Speaking tests to measure language proficiency.

Those scores are then averaged and rounded; the test maker then uses a confidential conversion table in order to produce a final Overall Band score. Scores can be reported in either whole or half bands. Each band corresponds to a descriptive statement that provides a summary of English competence.

The statements provided below will give you a sense of what competence is required for each band score. However, these are not the actual statements used by the test maker. For the actual descriptive statements for each band, please visit the official IELTS website, www.ielts.org.

Band 9: Expert User
Has complete control of the language: correct and effortless usage with complete understanding.

Band 8: Very Good User
Has complete control of the language with few errors. Confusion may take place in new or atypical circumstances. Is able to formulate advanced, in-depth arguments.

Band 7: Good User
Has advanced control of the language, though with a few errors or confusion in some circumstances. Uses sophisticated words and complex syntax, and comprehends dense arguments.

Band 6: Competent User
Has capable control of the language despite some errors and confusion. Can employ and comprehend moderately advanced language, but mainly in routine and typical circumstances.

Band 5: Modest User
Has limited control of the language. Is able to use plain statements in routine and typical circumstances. Commits numerous errors, and occasionally has difficultly with the general meaning of conversations.

Band 4: Limited User
Has low-level proficiency restricted to routine and typical circumstances. Uses only the most simplistic of words and syntax, and occasionally has trouble following a relatively simple, common conversation.

Band 3: Extremely Limited User

Cannot follow a relatively simple, common conversation, even with the most simplistic use of words and syntax.

Band 2: Intermittent User

Can handle only plain words to express basic needs. Even the most simple phrases or syntax usage are not well understood. Struggles significantly with spoken or written English.

Band 1: Non User

Knows a small number of random words. Has basically no understanding of English at all.

Candidates who do not attempt to answer any tasks score 0 for the test.

SCORING FOR THE LISTENING AND READING TESTS

In the IELTS Listening test, one mark is awarded for each correctly answered question. To obtain a band score of 7, you will need to answer at least 30 questions out of 40 correctly.

In the General or Academic Reading test, one mark is awarded for each correctly answered question. To get a band score of 7, you will need to answer at least 30 questions correctly.

Reading and Listening Answer Sheet

Only the answers transferred to the answer sheet are marked (see Figure 1 on page 21). The answers you write on the question paper during the test are not considered.

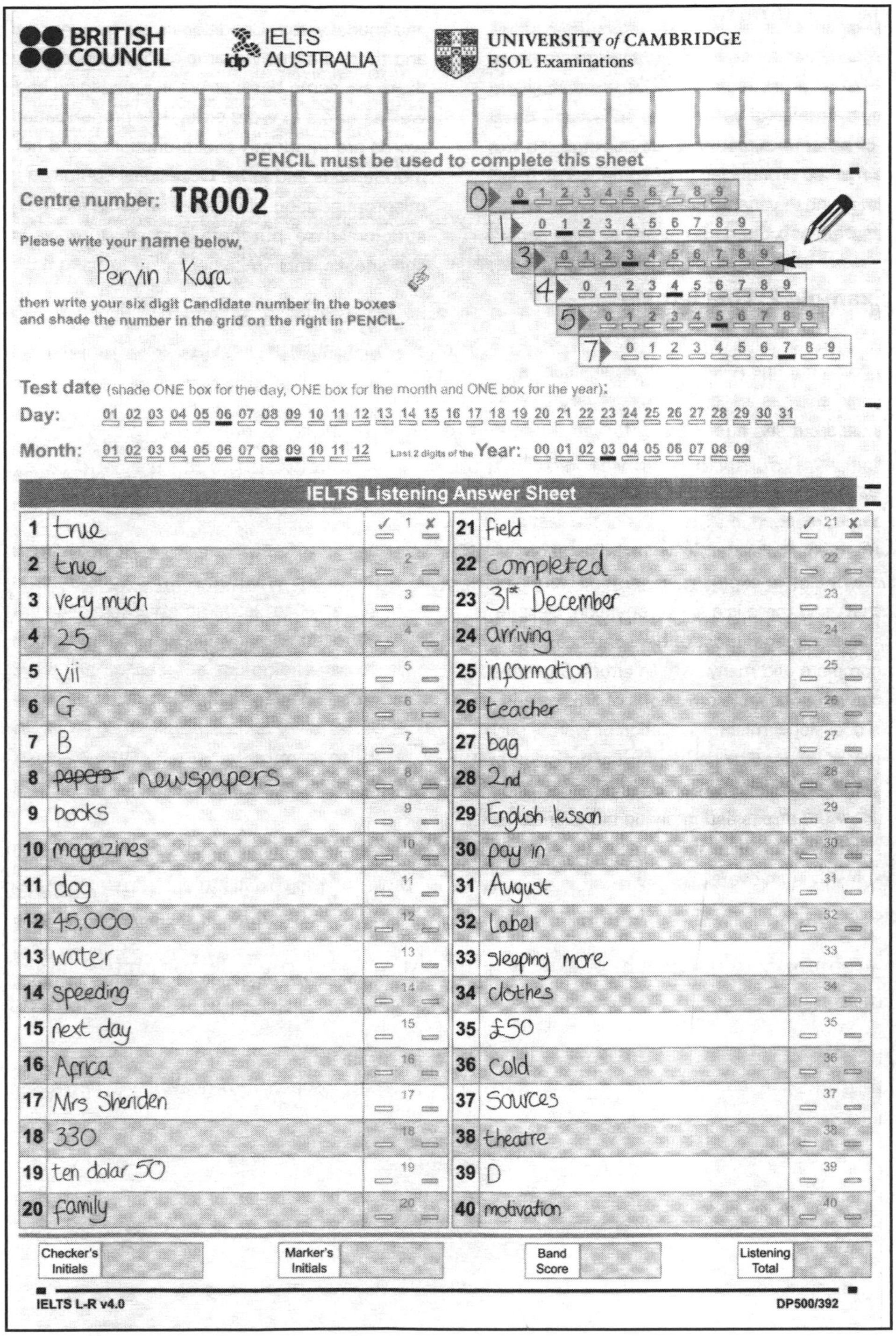

BRITISH COUNCIL   IELTS idp AUSTRALIA   UNIVERSITY of CAMBRIDGE ESOL Examinations

PENCIL must be used to complete this sheet

Centre number: TR002

Please write your name below,

Pervin Kara

then write your six digit Candidate number in the boxes and shade the number in the grid on the right in PENCIL.

0 1 3 4 5 7

Test date (shade ONE box for the day, ONE box for the month and ONE box for the year):

Day: 01 02 03 04 05 06 07 08 09 10 11 12 13 14 15 16 17 18 19 20 21 22 23 24 25 26 27 28 29 30 31

Month: 01 02 03 04 05 06 07 08 09 10 11 12   Last 2 digits of the Year: 00 01 02 03 04 05 06 07 08 09

IELTS Listening Answer Sheet

1	true	21	field
2	true	22	completed
3	very much	23	31st December
4	25	24	arriving
5	vii	25	information
6	G	26	teacher
7	B	27	bag
8	~~papers~~ newspapers	28	2nd
9	books	29	English lesson
10	magazines	30	pay in
11	dog	31	August
12	45.000	32	Label
13	water	33	sleeping more
14	speeding	34	clothes
15	next day	35	£50
16	Africa	36	cold
17	Mrs Sheriden	37	Sources
18	330	38	theatre
19	ten dolar 50	39	D
20	family	40	motivation

Checker's Initials   Marker's Initials   Band Score   Listening Total

IELTS L-R v4.0   DP500/392

Figure 1. Image Source: www.ielts.org

SCORING FOR WRITING AND SPEAKING TESTS

Your writing and speaking abilities will be assessed by various criteria.

Writing

There are two sets of criteria used to assess your writing. However, there are some differences in how the General Writing and the Academic Writing tasks are assessed.

- **General Training Writing Task 1**: You are asked to write a letter with a clear purpose that contains all the information specified in the task. Depending on the task, the letter will be written in either a formal or an informal style.

- **Academic Writing Task** 1: You are asked to write a report based on a table, graph or diagram. You need to report the data in the task accurately, and to identify and compare the key features.

- **General Training Writing and Academic Writing Task 2**: You are given a prompt in the form of a question or statement, and you are required to formulate and express your point of view on a subject. You must support your ideas with relevant examples from your own experience.

In addition to the above, both the General Training Writing and Academic Writing tests are marked using the following criteria:

- **Coherence and cohesion**: Your response needs to be logically organised into paragraphs, and you need to connect the ideas clearly. The paragraphs must have a central topic as well as supporting statements and examples.

- **Vocabulary**: To obtain a high score for this criterion, you must demonstrate a varied vocabulary. You need to be able to use the words appropriately and spell them correctly.

- **Grammatical range and accuracy**: You should use a variety of simple and complex grammatical structures accurately. You will also be assessed on your ability to punctuate your writing appropriately.

Speaking

Your speaking ability will be assessed by the following criteria:

- **Fluency and coherence**: Your ability to express ideas and opinions clearly and coherently, without long pauses and hesitations.

- **Lexical Resource**: Your ability to use a wide range of vocabulary naturally.

- **Grammatical range and accuracy**: Your ability to use a wide range of grammatical structures without making many mistakes.

- **Pronunciation**: Your ability to speak clearly and use pronunciation features naturally.

TEST RESULTS

You can collect your results 13 days after the test. You can either collect your certificate in person or authorise someone you know to do it for you. If requested, the results can be sent to you by mail. Test results cannot be given over the telephone, by fax or by email.

REGISTRATION

You can register to take the IELTS Test at your local authorised IELTS Test Centre. You can find information about IELTS Test Centres in your area, contact details and available dates using the database on the official IELTS webpage at www.ielts.org

How Do You Register?

Once you have chosen and contacted the IELTS Test Centre, you will receive the application form from the centre, which you will need to fill in and send or take to the centre with the test fee. You must attach two recent photos (no more than six months old).

You will be asked to write the number of your passport or national identity card on the application form, and attach a copy of the document. If you take the test outside your own country, your passport is the only valid form of identification.

The application must be fully completed to be processed. The centre will not process applications that are not complete. Once your application is processed, the centre will inform you in writing of the test venue, date and time when the test will take place.

Where Do You Take the IELTS?

The IELTS Test Centre will inform you of the test venue.

When Do You Take the IELTS?

There are 30–32 IELTS sessions in a calendar year. You can choose to register for any of the sessions 10–12 weeks in advance. It is recommended to register early to make sure you get a place on the date of your choice. The dates are fixed and cannot be changed. For a full list of the available dates at an IELTS test centre near you, please visit www.ielts.org.

How Much Does It Cost?

Test fees are set by IELTS Test Centres and may range from US$160 to US$220. You should contact your local centre for the exact fee.

WHAT TO EXPECT ON TEST DAY

On test day, you must arrive at the test venue 15 minutes before the test and show your identification to the IELTS Administrator. The identification you bring to the test must be the same as the identification you used to fill in the application form.

You will need to bring your own stationery (pencils, pens, a pencil sharpener and an eraser). You will not be allowed to take any bags, books or electronic devices (mobile phones, computers, recording devices, etc.).

The IELTS Administrator will check your identification and will take you to the examination room. You will be assigned a seat, which you will keep for the Listening, Reading and Writing tests.

You will be given the answer sheets to write your answers on. You may make notes on the question papers if you want, but you will not be allowed to take these out of the room.

The Speaking Test takes place at a different time and is usually on a different day. The test is recorded.

IELTS

PART 2:

STRATEGIES AND PRACTICE

CHAPTER 2: THE LISTENING MODULE

The Listening module consists of four recorded sections, each containing 10 questions, and takes about 30 minutes to complete. As you will hear the recording once only, success will depend on knowing what information to listen for. You are not expected to have any specialist knowledge, but you should be able to deal with a range of topics and a number of different voices and accents. Occasionally, IELTS recordings feature non-native English accents such as German or Spanish.

The test measures how well you can manage the following skills:

1. Listening for specific information
2. Listening for main ideas, supporting information and details
3. Understanding the speaker's opinion

THE LISTENING MODULE SECTIONS

Each of the four sections in the Listening module may have up to three different types of questions testing a combination of skills.

Before each section, you will hear a short introduction about the speaker(s) and the situation. This introduction is not printed on the question paper. You are then given time to look through the questions. There is also a break in the middle of sections 1, 2 and 3, giving you time to look at the questions in the second half.

Each section is heard once only and the questions always follow the order of the information presented in the recording. After each section, you are given 30 seconds to check your answers.

SECTION 1

Section 1 usually features a conversation concerning social needs, for example, an interview at an accommodation agency, or a survey. Typical question types that you may have to answer in this section are form completion, multiple choice and short answer. The target listening skill in this section is that of listening for specific information, for example, names, prices, measurements, etc.

The topic is usually social or general, and one speaker usually requires information from the other. The following are examples of conversations you may have to listen to in section 1:

- Answering the questions of customs/passport officials at the airport
- Asking a passer-by for directions to the nearest bank, post office, etc.
- Checking into a student residential college
- Making an appointment to meet a friend

SECTION 2

Section 2 usually concerns social and training needs. You will hear a monologue on a general, non-academic subject, for example, a short talk on how to use the local library facilities. Typical tasks found in this section are usually note/table/flow chart/sentence completion. The target listening skill is that of listening for main ideas and supporting points. The following are examples of monologues you may have to listen to in section 2:

- A library orientation talk
- A speech on healthy eating
- A talk about enrolment procedures at a fitness centre
- A radio broadcast about interesting places to visit in the area

SECTION 3

Section 3 is concerned with educational or training contexts. You will hear a conversation among up to four people, for example, a discussion between a tutor and a student, or several students discussing an assignment. Some typical tasks that can be found in this section are summary completion, diagram labelling, and matching. This section may test a range of skills, such as listening for specific information, main ideas and supporting points, and understanding a speaker's opinion. The following are examples of conversations you may hear in section 3:

- A conversation between a tutor and a student about completing an entry form for an engineer competition
- A group of students giving a presentation on an academic topic
- A job interview
- A discussion between a student and a tutor on how to complete a project

SECTION 4

Section 4, which is also concerned with educational and training contexts, will feature a monologue, for example, a lecture or talk of general, non-specialist academic interest. Some typical question types found in this section are matching, classification and multiple choice. As there is no break during this section, you must look through all the questions in the time given at the beginning. It is also especially important to listen for words signalling a change from one part of the lecture to another. The following are examples of monologues you may hear in section 4:

- A lecture on the radio about a health problem
- A university lecture about eclipses
- A monologue on how to breed animals
- A lecture about Neolithic Britain

LISTENING MODULE QUESTION TYPES

The question types in the Listening module consist of completion tasks; multiple choice; short answer; labelling a diagram, plan or map; classification; and matching.

Completion Tasks

- form completion
- note completion
- table completion
- flow chart completion
- summary completion
- sentence completion

Multiple Choice

- types of multiple choice
  - question and answer
  - unfinished Statement
- answer choice variations
  - three answer
  - four answer
  - more than four answer

Short Answer Questions

- direct answer
- lists

Labelling a diagram, plan, or map

- label a diagram plan, or map with words provided or from the audio

Classification

- place words or statements into given categories

Matching

- match items in two lists

COMPLETION TASKS

Completion tasks may include form completion, note completion, table completion, flow chart completion and summary or sentence completion.

Form Completion

Form completion tasks are usually found in section 1. You need to fill in missing information in the gaps. You have to listen for such specific information as names, dates, places, times, prices, measurements, special features and characteristics.

For questions involving things like measurements or money, you should write the unit of measurement (for example, cm, m, $) if this is not already given on the question paper. It is not necessary to write the full form (for example, centimetres); the abbreviated form or the symbol is fine. Such abbreviated forms (for example, 12m, $45, 23%) count as one word.

EXAMPLE: FORM COMPLETION

Questions 1 – 4

Complete the form below.

Write NO MORE THAN TWO WORDS AND/OR A NUMBER for each question.

PKT International Removals

Sales Consultant:		Andrew Smith
CONTACT DETAILS		
Contact person:		Bob Jones
Work number:		1 ....
Moving from:		35 Elm Street, Sydney
	Tel:	4656 5867
Moving to:	Country:	UK
	House/flat:	2 ....
	Street:	3 ....
	City:	4 ....

Note Completion

You complete notes by writing a specific number of words in the gap. In some cases, you are allowed to write no more than a certain number of words (and/or numbers), while in other cases they may be required to write an exact number of words (and/or numbers).

You complete the notes with the words you hear in the recording. Some of the information may already be written in the note.

Notes might not follow standard grammatical rules or layout. For example, there may be articles or auxiliary verbs missing, or a note may be a list with bullet points. Missing numbers in a note can be written in words or figures.

SAMPLE INSTRUCTIONS

Questions 12 – 14

Complete the notes below.

Write TWO WORDS for each answer.

or

Questions 12 – 14

Complete the notes below.

Write NO MORE THAN THREE WORDS AND/OR A NUMBER for each answer.

EXAMPLE: NOTE COMPLETION

Questions 12 – 14

Complete the notes below.

Write NO MORE THAN THREE WORDS AND/OR A NUMBER for each answer.

Assessed presentations

Audience:	**12** ……………............……. (no more than 30) plus tutor
Duration:	15 minutes
Date:	**13** ……………............…….
Topic:	Review of film, including
	a) background and director
	b) content **14** ……………............…….
	c) evaluation

Table Completion

You complete a table by writing words and/or numbers in the gaps provided. The number of words and/or numbers required or allowed will be clearly indicated in the instructions. The table will have several columns and each column will have a heading. The information is usually in note form, so you do not generally need to include words like articles or prepositions. Some of the information may already be given to help you. You only have to fill in the gaps in the columns and write the correct words and/or numbers on the answer sheet. Numbers can be written in words or figures. You should use no more than the number of words indicated in the instructions and make sure to spell them correctly.

EXAMPLE: TABLE COMPLETION

Questions 1 – 5

Complete the table below.

Write *NO MORE THAN THREE WORDS OR A NUMBER* for each answer.

KL School of English

Courses	Levels	Duration		Materials	Cost	Start date
Elementary	E1, E2, E3	45 hours	8 weeks	a coursebook and a **1**	$424	5 October
Pre-intermediate	P1, P2, P3					
Intermediate	I1, I2, I3					
Upper Intermediate	U1, U2, U3					
Advanced	A1, A2, A3					
Business English	B1, B2, B3	50 hours	**2** .... weeks	a coursebook and a set of **3**	$540	7 October
Preparation for proficiency exams	I	**4**	10 weeks		$550	**5** ....

Flow-chart Completion

Flow charts are used in the listening module to summarise a process or a sequence of events. As with all IELTS listening tasks, the information will always be given in chronological or logical order. You are required to complete the chart by writing words and/or numbers in the gaps. The number of words that you are required or allowed to use will be clearly stated in the instructions. Sometimes you are given a box of possible answers to choose from. If the items in the box are labelled A, B, C, etc., you will only write the appropriate letters in the spaces on their answer sheet. If no box with options is given, you write the required/allowed number of words you hear. Flow chart completion is similar to note completion in that it does not always follow standard grammatical rules or layout, that is, articles and auxiliary verbs may be omitted. You can write numbers in words or figures.

EXAMPLE: FLOW-CHART COMPLETION

Questions 15 – 17

Complete the chart below.

Write NO MORE THAN THREE WORDS AND/OR A NUMBER for each answer.

Recruitment Procedure at KL School of English

Candidate submits **15** ………….......…..... with ………..…........…….. .

↓

Candidate is informed of any **16** ………..…........……... missing in his application.

↓

Candidate is invited to an interview.

↓

Candidate is in interviewed by **17** ………..…........……...and senior teacher.

Summaries and Sentences

You are asked to complete sentences or a summary by writing words and/or numbers in gaps. The gaps can occur anywhere in the sentence. In listening, there is very little difference between sentence and summary completion. Sentences are joined together to form a summary. Sentence structure and the articles and prepositions in a summary or sentence are important and can be a useful guide to the missing words.

The word needed for the answer will always be in the recording. It should be written exactly as it is heard, for example, without changing from plural to singular. The completed sentences must be grammatically correct. If the word you choose is not grammatically correct, you have chosen the wrong answer. For example:

- It is important to eat a _...balance..._diet.

In this example, the candidate failed to hear '-ed' at the end of the word and wrote 'balance'. However, 'balance' is not the correct answer for two reasons: (1) this is not what the speaker actually said, and (2) it does not fit into this sentence grammatically. The correct answer is 'balanced'.

EXAMPLE: SENTENCE OR SUMMARY COMPLETION

Questions 15 – 19

Complete the sentences below.

Write NO MORE THAN THREE WORDS AND/OR A NUMBER for each answer.

15 The audience for the event is expected to wear a ....…..

16 If you want to take children to the venue, you must ....….

17 The band will perform at ....… o'clock.

18 To get a full programme of the event, you should ....….

MULTIPLE CHOICE

You must choose the correct answer to a question from a list of answer choices.

Types of Multiple Choice Questions

There are two sub-types of multiple choice questions, and both types can appear together in the same set of questions.

QUESTION AND ANSWER

Where does Jenny decide to put her MP3 player?

- **A** In the handbag
- **B** In the box
- **C** In storage with the furniture

UNFINISHED STATEMENT

The meeting was scheduled for

- **A** 2.30 p.m.
- **B** 3.30 p.m.
- **C** 4.30 p.m.
- **D** 7.30 p.m.

Answer Choice Variations

There are three different types of answer choice variations for a multiple choice question.

As with all multiple choice questions in the IELTS exam, you only need to write the letter of your answer choice on the answer sheet.

THREE ANSWER CHOICES: A, B AND C

Question 31

Choose the correct letters, A, B or C.

According to the doctor, the main cause of back pain in women is

   A   pregnancy.

   B   osteoporosis.

   C   lack of exercise.

FOUR ANSWER CHOICES: A, B, C AND D

Question 32

Choose the correct letter, A, B, C or D.

The noise levels at the site can reach

   A   45 decibels.

   B   50 decibels.

   C   65 decibels.

MORE THAN FOUR ANSWER CHOICES

Question 12

Choose TWO letters, A – E.

Which two groups of patients receive free medication?

   A   People over 16 years old

   B   Unemployed people

   C   Non-US residents

   D   People over 55 years old

KAPLAN)

SHORT-ANSWER QUESTIONS

Short-answer questions focus on understanding main ideas and factual information. You are required to answer questions using words and/or numbers. The number of words and/or numbers you are required or allowed to use will be clearly indicated in the instructions. There are two variations of short-answer questions.

1. DIRECT ANSWER: VARIATION 1 IS WHERE YOU ANSWER A DIRECT QUESTION.

Question 16

What is the main cause of earthquakes?

....

2. LISTS: VARIATION 2 IS WHERE YOU MAKE A LIST OF UP TO THREE THINGS.

Questions 17 – 19

Write NO MORE THAN ONE WORD for each answer.

List THREE factors which affect the speed of biodegrading.

17   ....…......................

18   ....…......................

19   ....…......................

It is important to read the instructions very carefully to know what is required for an answer to score a point. Sometimes you are required to give two answers to score one mark. That is, if you give only one answer or one of the two answers is wrong, you will not get a point for the question attempted. In other cases, you will get a point for each correct answer in the list.

In the example below, you will get one mark for each correct answer.

Questions 20 – 22

Write NO MORE THAN TWO WORDS for each answer.

Name THREE things that the students are required to submit with their application.

20   ....…......................

21   ....…......................

22   ....…......................

In the example below, you will get only one mark for two correct answers.

Question 23

According to the lecture, which TWO animals depend on their acoustic sense to find prey?

…………......................

…………......................

EXAMPLE: SHORT-ANSWER QUESTIONS

Questions 3 – 6

Write NO MORE THAN ONE WORD for each answer.

List FOUR factors that affect migration to cities.

   3 …………...............………

   4 …………...............………

   5 …………...............………

   6 …………...............………

LABELLING A DIAGRAM, PLAN OR MAP

You are required to label the parts on a diagram using words and/or numbers. The number of words and/or numbers required or allowed is clearly indicated in the instructions. The parts to be labelled have an arrow and the question number beside them. There may be a box of possible answers labelled **A**, **B**, **C**, etc., to choose from. In this case, you are only required to write the correct letters in the appropriate spaces on your answer sheet. If there is no box with options given, write the words you hear in the recording.

EXAMPLE: LABELLING A DIAGRAM, PLAN OR MAP

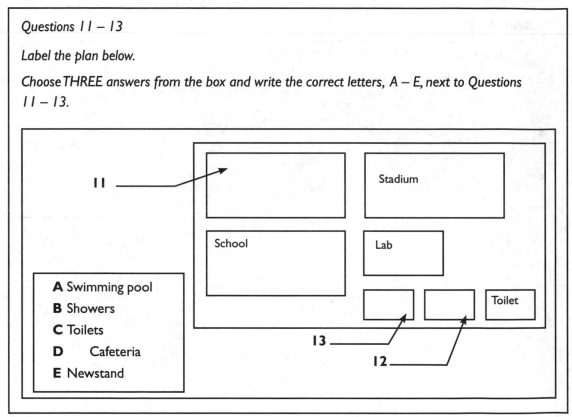

Questions 11 – 13

Label the plan below.

Choose THREE answers from the box and write the correct letters, A – E, next to Questions 11 – 13.

CLASSIFICATION

You are required to decide which category several words or statements belong to. The categories are usually labelled **A**, **B**, **C**, etc. The words or statements are usually labelled with the question numbers.

As with all IELTS listening tasks, the questions usually follow the order in which you hear the information. Based on what you hear, you must match the words or ideas in the questions to one of the categories. Since there are more questions than categories, you may choose the category letters more than once, as in the example on the next page.

EXAMPLE: CLASSIFICATION

Questions 21 – 26

According to the speaker, in which situation are the following media most useful?

A Individual learners

B Seven or eight learners

C Whole group

Write the correct letter, A, B or C, next to Questions 21 – 26. You may choose any letter more than once.

21	Computers	....	24	Flipcharts	....
22	Videos	....	25	Audio CDs	....
23	Books	....	26	Interactive whiteboards	....

MATCHING

You are required to match items in a list (numbered **1**, **2**, **3**, etc.) to the correct word or phrase in a box (labelled **A**, **B**, **C**, etc.). Some of the items in the box may have to be used more than once, while other items might not have a match in the list. You must match the correct option to each question based on what you hear. As in the example below, you are only required to write the correct letter in the appropriate spaces on your answer sheet.

You should be aware that in matching tasks, the words and phrases in the box are usually all mentioned, but not always in the order they are given in the text, and some of them may never be used to answer any of the questions. The questions follow the order in which the information is given in the listening text.

EXAMPLE: MATCHING

Questions 1 – 4

What recommendations does the tutor give about the items on the reading list?

Choose your answers from the box and write the correct letter, A – E, next to Questions 1 – 4.

1	Smith	....
2	Brown	....
3	Jackson	....
4	Johnson	....

A	useful
B	read introduction
C	read conclusion
D	essential
E	unnecessary

LISTENING MODULE STRATEGIES: ALL SECTIONS

The strategies below refer to skills that are important when you are listening during the IELTS test.

> ## Strategy 1: Listen actively.

One of the major challenges that you, as an IELTS candidate, have to face is doing several things while listening. You must recognise more than just names, places and times. You must also connect ideas, organise information, generalise and infer.

Here are 'active listening' strategies that you can use for all Listening module question types.

BEFORE YOU LISTEN

- *Read the instructions to know how many words you are allowed or required to write.*
  The word limit includes all words, including articles and prepositions. Do not go above the word limits or your answer will be marked incorrect.

- *Read through the questions and notes on the question paper and decide what the topic is.*
  For example, to get the right information from a conversation or monologue, it helps if you ask yourself the right questions before you begin listening, such as:

  - Who is talking?
  - What are they talking about?
  - How do they feel about it?

- *Analyse the questions and prompts, and decide what type of information is required.*
  This may include information such as a price, name or time.

- *Consider the options in relation to the question.* In some cases, an option may be true, but does not answer the question.

- *Eliminate options* by putting a cross beside them when you are sure they are wrong.

- *Underline the key words* in the rubric, questions and options before you listen. Underlining or highlighting the key words around each gap in completion tasks—or in questions in other tasks—can help you listen more effectively.

  For example, a speaker might use vocabulary that helps you identify how the talk is organised. Say a professor is giving a lecture on Newton's laws of physics. She might discuss each law using 'first', 'next', 'then', 'finally', etc. as follows:

  - Body paragraph 1: 'Isaac Newton **first** thought that…. He tested this theory by…. His observations showed….'

  - Body paragraph 2: '**Next**, Newton had always believed…. He conducted an experiment that…. **Then** he saw how….'

  - Body paragraph 3: '**Finally**, Newton theorized that…. However, when he learned that….'

- *Mouth the options in the box quietly to yourself,* that is, form the words with your mouth, but do not speak them out loud. This may help you recognise them in the recording.

- *Try to re-phrase the notes and questions in your own words.* This could help you identify the moment when the speaker is about to give the correct answer.

- *Try to re-phrase the possible answers in your own words* because the speakers might give the correct answer using parallel expressions.

WHILE YOU LISTEN

- *Listen for any clue that the speakers are about to answer the questions.* They will probably use different words from the question.

- *Always choose only the required number of options for each question.*

- *Do not write more than the maximum number of words you are asked for.* Write only the words that you hear, without changing them.

- *If you miss an answer, do not worry—keep listening.* Otherwise, you will miss the next question, too.

AFTER YOU LISTEN

- *Make sure you answer every question* because you will not lose marks for wrong answers.

- *As you copy your answers, check that the words you have written make sense* in the context, are grammatically correct and are correctly spelt.

- *Do not copy anything printed on the question paper when transferring your answers to the answer sheet.* You should copy what you have written yourself.

NUMBER CONVENTIONS

When you listen for specific information, you are listening for key, factual information. In many completion tasks in the IELTS listening test, you have to listen for numbers. You should be familiar with the following conventions:

Telephone Numbers

These are usually spoken as individual numbers. For example, 273458 would be spoken as 'two seven three four five eight'. With seven-digit numbers, speakers often divide them into one group of three and one group of four, with a short pause between the groups. For example, 634-4398 would be spoken as 'six three four... four three nine eight'.

Sometimes a few numbers are grouped into a larger number, especially when this involves consecutive zeros. For example, the number 975600 would be spoken as 'nine seven five six hundred'.

Often, '0' in telephone numbers is spoken as the letter 'o', as in 'go'. In British and Australian English, sometimes the words 'double' and 'triple' are used. For example, the phone number 334-6777 would be spoken as 'double three four ... six triple seven'.

Decimal Numbers

Decimal numbers are introduced with the word 'point' and then each decimal number is spoken individually. For example, the number 16.78 would be spoken as 'sixteen point seven eight'.

Prices

When talking about prices, the word 'point' is not usually used. The decimal numbers are usually combined and introduced with 'and'. For example, $15.75 would be spoken as 'fifteen dollars and seventy-five cents'. Sometimes, the currency is also left out. For example, $15.75 would be spoken as 'fifteen seventy-five'.

Fractions

With the exception of 'a half', 'a quarter', and 'a third', fractions are expressed with 'th' at the end. For example, the fraction 7/8 would be spoken as 'seven-eighths' and 9/10 would be spoken as 'nine-tenths'.

Thousands

It is also possible to express thousands as the equivalent number of hundreds. For example, 1,700 would be spoken as 'seventeen hundred'; 2,700 would be spoken as 'twenty-seven hundred'; and 1,123 would be spoken as 'eleven hundred and twenty-three'.

Dates

There are several possible ways to write dates. In British English, the day comes before the month, and periods are often used to separate elements. For example, the date May 16, 1976 would be written 16.05.76 or 16.5.1976. In American English, the month comes first, and slashes are often used to separate elements. For example, May 16, 1976 would be written 05/16/76 or 5/16/1976.

For the IELTS listening test, you should adhere to the following format:

- 5 July
- 5 July 2004 (when it is necessary to include the year)

> ## Strategy 2: Anticipate key points based on the main idea.

Anticipating means thinking about what might or will come next. Anticipation makes listening easier. Knowing the topic helps you predict and anticipate certain details. For example, a student who wants to talk about his term paper might have problems with the topic, organisation, due date, length, bibliography or a partner. Similarly, a professor who gives a lecture on bees might discuss their appearance, abilities, evolution, migration, reproduction, diet, reasons for studying them, and so on. Knowing the possibilities makes it easier to hear what the speaker says.

bibliography

> ## Strategy 3: Do not try to record everything in notes.

If you decide to take notes during the exam, you need to make sure they are effective and efficient. That means you need to determine the topic of the talk, study the questions, decide what type of information and what types of words are missing. Based on your observations, focus on noting down only those words. While making notes, less important words could either be omitted or recorded using symbols and abbreviations.

For example, say an essential topic of the talk is a project that started in 1996. The key words to remember would be 'project', 'started' and '1996'. It is very unlikely that in the IELTS exam you will be asked to complete a gap with 'started' or 'the'. Therefore, you could make the following notes: 'project: →1996'

When you are given 30 seconds at the end of each section to check your answers, look at your notes and circle the parts that you think answer the questions.

LISTENING MODULE STRATEGIES FOR CONVERSATIONS, LECTURES AND TALKS

The following strategies refer to strategies that are particularly important when you listen to a conversation, lecture or talk during the IELTS listening examination.

> ## Strategy 1: Create one column for each speaker in your notes to avoid confusion when you read them.

Should you decide to make notes, it is important to keep them organised. To do this, create one column for each speaker in the conversation. Although names are useful, you will never be asked to name any of the speakers. So depending on the type of conversation, identify each speaker as Professor and Student, Man and Woman, or Student 1 and Student 2.

> ## Strategy 2: Be prepared for the unique elements of spoken English.

The speakers in the listening test will not sound as if they are reading an essay. Instead, their speech will be natural and resemble everyday spoken English, which can include interruptions and self-correction.

INTERRUPTIONS

An interruption occurs when a listener in a conversation or lecture says something before the speaker has finished making a point or observation. A speaker could be interrupted by a question or comment, and the speaker will have to resolve the interruption before returning to the original topic. You will have to remember what was said before the interruption to understand fully what is said after. Some common vocabulary for interruptions includes:

- 'Excuse me, but…'
- 'I'm sorry, but…'
- 'I don't want to be rude, but…'
- 'Hold on…'
- 'Hang on…'
- 'Can I interrupt?'
- 'Can I just say that…'

SELF-CORRECTION

Anyone, even a lecturer, can misspeak (speak incorrectly), often by using the wrong word. When people misspeak, they interrupt themselves and then restate their idea correctly. Self-correction could involve some of the following key words or expressions:

- 'Actually…'
- 'Hang on…'
- 'Hold on…'
- 'That's not exactly right.'
- 'That's not really true.'
- 'Let me rephrase that.'
- 'Let me start again/start over.'

Such mistakes are usually used in the listening examination as distracters. That is, you hear the incorrect information and think it is the correct answer. Once they note it down, they start listening for the answer to the next question, thus losing a point. It is important to be aware of this sort of distracter and be prepared to change your answers accordingly.

Strategy 3: Be prepared to infer.

Even though it is possible, a speaker will probably not state how his or her talk is organised directly. Therefore, do not rely on an explicit, obvious statement such as 'Let's organise our discussion by types of energy sources' or 'I want to begin with the best solution and then continue to the least suitable.' You will probably have to recognise how the passage is organised on your own.

LISTENING MODULE PRACTICE SECTIONS

In this section, you will find four Listening module practice sections. You can write your answers and make notes the pages in the book. Note that in the real test you will be given time to transfer your answers from the question paper with the listening tasks to a separate answer sheet.

GO ON TO THE NEXT PAGE

 LISTENING PRACTICE SECTION 1

Questions 1 – 5

*Choose the correct letter, **A**, **B**, or **C**.*

1   Which of the statements is true?

The candidate

   A   needs to take the IELTS General module.
   B   needs to take the IELTS Academic module.
   C   is not sure which module he needs to take.

2   On which days would the candidate like to take the exam on?

   A   The same day
   B   Different days
   C   Weekends

3   The Listening, Reading and Writing Tests take place on

   A   Tuesdays.
   B   Thursdays.
   C   Saturdays.

4   What kind of ID can the candidate **NOT** use?

   A   A driving licence
   B   A library card
   C   A passport

5   The candidate will do the Listening, Reading and Writing tests

   A   without breaks.
   B   with one-hour breaks between the tests.
   C   with 15-minute breaks between the tests.

KAPLAN

Questions 6 – 10

Complete the notes below. Write NO MORE THAN THREE WORDS for each answer.

IELTS Test Contact Information and Details

Number of days to get results: **6** ....13............

Test fee: **7** US$ ....200............

Send documents registered mail to: Exams Administrator

47 Clover Place

8 ....new ROCHDLLE............

New York

9 Zip: ....40806............

Contact email: inquiry@examsmail.com

Contact telephone number: **10** ....365 9082............

LISTENING PRACTICE SECTION 2

Questions 1 – 2

Choose the correct letter, **A, B, C** *or* **D**.

1   What does Mark think about time management?

    A   It is a subject he would like to talk about.

    B   It is something he does not know much about.

    C   It is something he is not good at.

    D   It is a subject he does not like talking about.

2   What does Mark say about the presentation?

    A   He has planned the outline.

    B   He hasn't started planning it yet.

    C   He has thought about which ideas to include.

    D   He needs to change some parts of it.

Questions 3 – 10

When is Mark giving the presentation?　　3 …………………..........

Complete the list. Write *NO MORE THAN THREE WORDS* for your answer.

Time Management Presentation

Introduction:

Start with a general statement

Main part:

Common Problems:

4 …………………............ things, for example, last minute holiday shopping

Relying too much on 5 ……*memory*………

Improving time management skills:

- Make to-do lists
- 6 ……*plan the time*………
- Break down projects into 7 ……*small parts*………
- Setting 8 ……*deadline*………
- Dealing with 9 ……*presentation*………
- Using the word 10 ……*interruption* NO………

LISTENING PRACTICE SECTION 3

Questions 1 – 3

Choose THREE letters, A – E.

Which *THREE* of the following does Peter discuss?

(A) The effects of sleep deprivation on health
(B) The effects technology on sleeping patterns
C How to deal with sleep problems
(D) Comparing sleep patterns now with the past
E Sleep and long distance travel

1 ....

2 ....

3 ....

Questions 4 – 5

Label the parts of the pie chart.

Choose your answers from the box on the right.

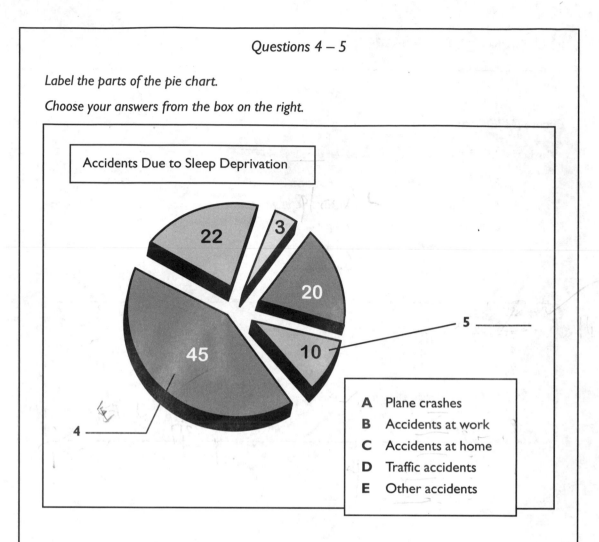

Accidents Due to Sleep Deprivation

A	Plane crashes
B	Accidents at work
C	Accidents at home
D	Traffic accidents
E	Other accidents

Questions 6 – 10

Complete the list of the recommendations.

Write NO MORE THAN ONE WORD for each answer.

To sleep better:

Do's	Don'ts
Find out how much sleep you need (on holiday or long weekends) Improve the quality of sleep: • Have a warm shower or 6 ...bath... before going to bed. • Do quiet activities such as reading or 7 ...filling.... • Have a warm drink • Consider taking up yoga or 8 ...mediatation	Don't use technology late at night. Don't eat late. Avoid drinking 9 ...coffee... and energy drinks. Don't do intense 10 ...physical excercise

🎧 LISTENING PRACTICE SECTION 4

Questions 1 – 5

Listen to a lecture on successful language learning.

Write NO MORE THAN THREE WORDS for each answer.

Factors for Successful Language Learning	
A **Exposure** to target language determines 1 ....*speed of learning*..........	
B **Motivation**	
2 ....*instrumental*.... **motivation** Language is a tool to achieve practical goals, for example, getting a job or 3 ...*passing an examination*...	**Integrative motivation** Language is a tool for socialising and integrating, for example, 4 .... or people who are married to speakers of another language.
According to research, integrative motivation produces 5 ...*much better results*...	

(handwritten margin notes: "what makes", "instrumental", "immigrants")

Questions 6 – 10

Write NO MORE THAN TWO WORDS for each answer.

C   Personality

Good language learners are willing to take **6** ....*risks*........ are not afraid of making mistakes and try to **7** ....*learn*........ with the language.

D   Learning Systems

- Efficient **8** ....*revision technique link*........
- Systems for organising and learning vocabulary
- Ability to monitor one's own speech
- Ability to plan learning

E   Age

Children learn faster than adults.

Adult learners can be successful if they

- are aware of how they learn
- are independent of **9** ....*Teachers*........
- take **10** ....*responsibility*........ for learning

meditation

ANSWERS AND EXPLANATIONS

The portions of the audio that are applicable to each question are included here. The key words needed to select the correct answer are highlighted in **bold**.

LISTENING PRACTICE SECTION I

1 (C)	Script –	...I'll have to contact the university to find out **just to make sure ...**
2 (A)	Script –	...it would be more **convenient** to do all the papers **on the same day** ...
3 (C)	Script –	...Reading, Writing and Listening tests take place **on Saturdays** ...
4 (B)	Script –	...We only accept **original passports** and national IDs...
5 (A)	Script –	...I'm afraid **there aren't any breaks** between the papers ...
6 (13)	Script –	...It takes 13 calendar days ...
7 (200)	Script –	...The examination fee is **US$200.**
8 (New Rochelle)	Script –	...N-E-W-R-O-C-H-E-L-L-E.
9 (10806)	Script –	...zip code is 10806 ...
10 (3259082)	Script –	...phone us at 3259082 ...

LISTENING PRACTICE SECTION 2

1 (C)		Script – ...I'm probably the **worst student when it comes to time management.**
2 (C)		Script – ...I just **don't know where to start** ...
3 (Friday / Friday, 10.00 a.m.)		Script – ...the presentation is **scheduled for 10.00 a.m. this Friday.**
4 (putting off)		Script – ...One of the common problems is **putting** things **off**.
5 (memory)		Script – ...relying too much on your **memory** ...
6 (prioritise)		Script – ...Another way to deal with the problem is to **prioritise** ...
7 (smaller parts/tasks)		Script – ...I should break big projects into **small parts with a specific goal.**
8 (deadlines)		Script – ...I think setting **deadlines** and sticking to them ...
9 (interruptions)		Script – ...blocking in time to handle unpredictable **interruptions** ...
10 (no/No)		Script – ...Saying **'No'**, which is one of the most useful words in English ...

LISTENING PRACTICE SECTION 3

Answers 1 – 3 can be in any order: B D A, A D B, etc.

1 **(B)**	Script – ...Many researchers **link** sleep deprivation with **electricity, television, and computers** ...
2 **(D)**	Script – ...**Before** electricity was invented ... By **1975** ... and **today** ...
3 **(A)**	Script – ...a variety of **physical and psychological problems** ...
4 **(D)**	Script – ...**45% of all traffic accidents**
5 **(C)**	Script – ...**10% of domestic accidents**
6 **(bath)**	Script – ...have a warm shower or **bath** ...
7 **(filing)**	Script – ...Doing some **quiet activities** such as reading or **filing** ...
8 **(meditation)**	Script – ...Some people take up yoga or **meditation** to help them relax ...
9 **(Caffeine-rich drinks)**	Script – ...**Caffeine-rich drinks** increase your heart rate ...
10 **(physical exercise)**	Script – ...The same goes for vigorous **physical exercise** ...

caffeine

LISTENING PRACTICE SECTION 4

1 **(speed of learning)**   Script – ...It's this factor which determines **the speed of learning a language** …

2 **(Instrumental)**   Script – ...Research into motivation has identified two main types: **instrumental** motivation and integrative motivation …

3 **(passing an examination)**   Script – ...practical reasons, such as getting a job or **passing an examination** …

4 **(Immigrants)**   Script – ...**Immigrants** or people who are married to speakers of another language are motivated in this way.

5 **([much] better results …)**   Script – ...integrative motivation produces **much better results** …

6 **(risks)**   Script – ...willingness to experiment and take **risks** is essential.

7 **(experiment)**   Script – ...Good language learners will **try to experiment** with different ways of learning …

8 **(revision techniques)**   Script – ...They develop their own learning style and use a range of learning skills such as efficient **revision techniques** …

9 **(teacher)**   Script – ...make decisions about their learning and are **independent of the teacher** …

10 **(responsibility)**   Script – ...aware of how they learn, and who **take responsibility** for their learning …

CHAPTER 3: THE READING MODULE

The Reading module is the second part of the IELTS examination. It lasts 60 minutes and consists of 40 questions based on a variety of task types. You need to read three or four passages—about 2,000-2,750 words in total. There are usually three passages in the Academic Reading module, and three or four passages in the General Training Reading module. You are not given extra time at the end of the reading test to transfer your answers to the answer sheet. Answers need to be written on the answer sheet in the 60 minutes given to complete the Reading module.

The IELTS Reading module tests a range of skills, such as skimming and scanning, understanding main ideas, reading for detail and understanding opinion and attitude.

DIFFERENCES BETWEEN ACADEMIC AND GENERAL TRAINING READING MODULES

While the task types of the Academic and General Training Reading modules are the same, the types of reading passages differ. The Academic module will usually contain at least one passage organised as a logical argument, while the readings in the General Training module are likely to be more descriptive or instructive. The organisation of non-argumentative texts may vary, but common organisational themes are categories, chronological description and describing a process.

The Academic Reading module involves reading three passages, with one passage per section. Texts come from books, magazines, newspapers and journals, and are non-specialist. At least one passage contains a detailed argument. Although the texts are representative of reading requirements for undergraduate and postgraduate students, they are not discipline specific. The passages are usually presented in increasing order of difficulty.

The General Training Reading module involves reading three or four passages grouped into three or four sections. Section 1 usually deals with social survival. It consists of one or two texts that are short but contain a lot of information—for example, public information leaflets. Section 2 focuses on subjects related to general training, and usually consists of two texts which, for example, give information about a university or college and services or facilities provided. Sections 3 and 4 consist of one longer text each related to general training, and involve general reading comprehension on almost any subject.

Each section in the General Training Reading module has 8–15 questions, and each section in the Academic Reading module has 13–15 questions.

READING MODULE QUESTION TYPES

The question types in the Reading module comprise multiple-choice questions; short-answer questions; sentence and summary completion; note completion; table completion; flow-chart completion; labelling a diagram; matching; true/false/not given; yes/no/not given; and classification.

Multiple Choice

- single answer - choose one of up to four options
- multiple answer - choose more than one answer from a list of options

Short Answer Questions

- direct answer
- lists

Completion Tasks

- note completion
- table completion
- flow chart completion
- summary completion
- sentence completion

Labelling a diagram

- Label a diagram with words from a passage

Matching

- match items in two lists
- match text or visual information to each other or other texts

True/False/Not Given

- compare statements to information in the passage and decide if they agree, disagree, or the information is not given

Yes/No/Not Given

- compare statements to information in the passage and decide if they agree, disagree, or the information is not given

Classification

- place words or statements into given categories

MULTIPLE-CHOICE QUESTIONS

Multiple-choice questions may focus on main ideas, details or the writer's opinion. There are multiple-choice questions with a single answer and multiple-choice questions with multiple answers.

In the single-answer type, you are asked to choose one answer from up to four possible options; in the multiple-answer type, you are asked to choose more than one answer from a longer list of possible options. In this case, your answers do not have to be in alphabetical order. For example, D, A, C and A, C, D are both considered the same.

Multiple-choice questions always follow the order of the information in the passage, and may cover one section of the passage, or the whole passage. The options, on the other hand, do not necessarily follow the order of information in the passage. The questions and options are usually paraphrased information from the passage.

EXAMPLE: MULTIPLE-CHOICE QUESTIONS

Questions 21 and 22

Choose the correct letters, **A – D**.

21   According to the passage, cats are very good at

      A   hiding their tracks.

      B   hunting at night.

      C   spotting their prey at night.

      D   hunting in groups.

22   According to the passage, which **TWO** of the following are typical of cat's hunting behaviour?

      A   They hunt in short bursts of intense exercise punctuating long periods of rest.

      B   They hunt using tactics similar to those of leopards and tigers.

      C   They like to share excess prey with others in their group.

      D   They like to present their prey to their owners or other cats.

      E   They mainly use ambush tactics while hunting.

SHORT-ANSWER QUESTIONS

In the IELTS Reading module, short-answer questions usually focus on factual information. The questions reflect the order of information in the text, but the answers may be widely spaced in the text, so you need to use key words in the questions to help you scan the text quickly. Your answers do not need to be complete sentences and must not exceed the stated number of words. You do not usually need to include words like articles or auxiliary verbs.

You should study the questions and identify the relevant parts of the text, then scan each of these parts for possible answers. You must not change the form of the words or use different words—the answers must come directly from the passage.

EXAMPLE: SHORT-ANSWER QUESTIONS

Questions 13 and 14

Answer the following questions.

Write NO MORE THAN THREE WORDS AND/OR A NUMBER for each answer.

Write your answers in boxes 13 and 14 on your answer sheet.

13   How long does the Marine Biology course last?   ....

14   When does the postgraduate programme end?   ....

SENTENCE AND SUMMARY COMPLETION

In sentence and summary completion tasks, the questions reflect the order of information in the text. The sentences and the summary will focus on key information from part or all of the passage. There are two kinds of sentence and summary completion tasks. You may be asked to complete a sentence or summary by taking words directly from the text or by choosing from a list of options.

EXAMPLE: SENTENCE AND SUMMARY COMPLETION

Questions 1 – 3

Complete the sentences below with words taken from the reading passage.

Write NO MORE THAN THREE WORDS for each answer.

1   To make a .... , you should study your options well.

2   You shouldn't choose a position simply because it has ....

3   You might want to do more studies to improve your ....

NOTE COMPLETION

Note completion tasks usually focus on the main ideas of part or all of the text. They may include headings, subheadings and numbers or bullet points. In note completion tasks, you may have to complete gapped notes by using a bank of answers in a box.

The words provided in the box might not be the same as the words in the text. You should look for parallel meanings in the text, for example, 'political unrest' in the notes could be 'political events' in the text. Notes might not follow standard grammatical rules or layout; there may be articles or auxiliary verbs missing. Some of the information might already be written in the note.

EXAMPLE: NOTE COMPLETION

Questions 35 and 36

Complete the missing information.

Use NO MORE THAN THREE WORDS for each answer.

The construction of the local City Hall

1836	Design for building chosen by **35** ………….................. .
1838	Work halted by political unrest in the country.
1839	Work resumed.
1840	Work stopped when **36** ………….................. .
1841	Work resumed.
1842	Building completed.

TABLE COMPLETION

You are required to complete gaps in a table using the stated number of words from the passage. Some of the information may already be provided to help you. As with other completion tasks in the IELTS Reading module, the questions reflect the order of information in the text.

In this task, you are often tested on your knowledge of synonyms and paraphrases. For example, Question 12 below asks if experience is 'necessary' for each of the jobs. In the text, it may say that experience is 'essential'.

EXAMPLE: TABLE COMPLETION

Questions 12 and 13

Complete the table below.

Write NO MORE THAN THREE WORDS AND/OR A NUMBER for each answer.

Position	Salary	Experience necessary
Secretary	$500 per month	No
Teacher	$1,500 per month	12 …………..................
Senior Teacher	$2,000 per month	Yes
Director of Studies	13 $ ………….................	Yes

FLOW-CHART COMPLETION

Flow charts are used to summarise the different steps in a series of events or a process. Although the information will be given in chronological order in the flow chart, it might not follow the order of the information in the text. You need to study the flow chart carefully and use the keywords to identify the relevant part(s) of the text. While reading the part(s) carefully, you should reconstruct the chronological order in which the events happen and complete the flow chart.

EXAMPLE: FLOW-CHART COMPLETION

Questions 9 – 11

Complete the flow chart.

Write NO MORE THAN THREE WORDS for each answer.

> Candidates complete an application form and send it with **9** ………….................. .

⬇

> Candidates receive 'Induction Pack' which contains:
>
> - A psychological evaluation form
> - Instructions on **10** …………..................

⬇

> Candidates receive full details of their placement.

LABELLING A DIAGRAM

Passages that describe mechanical devices or processes may include a diagram-labelling task (example provided on next page). A diagram-labelling task may relate to one section of the text or to several paragraphs. This task requires you to read the paragraphs carefully and study the diagram at the same time. Some labels may already be provided to help you.

You should pay particular attention to locating specific words that form part of the labels in the diagram and be careful to copy the words you need accurately from the passage. It is helpful to keep in mind that labels on the diagram are generally ordered in a clockwise direction, which will not necessary reflect the order in which the information appears in the text.

EXAMPLE: LABELLING A DIAGRAM

Questions 21 – 24

Label the diagram below.

Choose NO MORE THAN TWO WORDS from the passage for each answer.

The Mouse

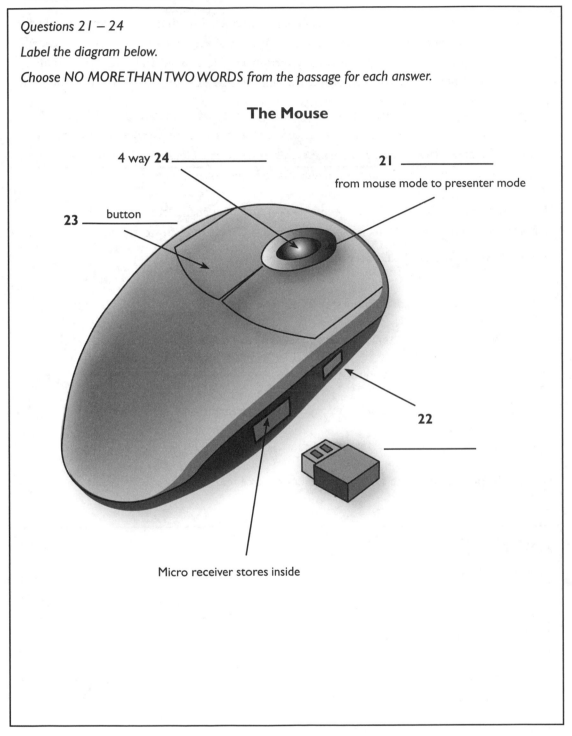

4 way **24** _____

21 _____

from mouse mode to presenter mode

23 _____ button

22 _____

Micro receiver stores inside

MATCHING

There is a wide variety of matching tasks used in the IELTS Reading module. You may be asked to match pieces of textual or visual information to each other or to sections of a text. In the Academic Training module, these sections will be paragraphs from a single passage. In the General Training module, you might have a selection of shorter texts rather than a single passage. For example, you might be asked to match pictures or statements to advertisements.

EXAMPLE 1: MATCHING

> *Questions 5 – 10*
>
> *Look at statements* **5 – 10** *and advertisements* **A – C***. Match each statement with the advertisement it applies to. Write the correct letter,* **A – C***, next to each statement.*
>
> **NB**   *You may use any letter more than once.*
>
> 5   The job is not for those interested in full-time positions.   .....C....
>
> 6   The job offers opportunities for professional development.   .....A....
>
> 7   The job requires communication skills.   .....C....
>
> 8   The position requires a previous psychological evaluation.   .....B....
>
> 9   The position requires experience in sales.   .....C....
>
> 10   The post is offered to skilled and experienced candidates only.   .....A....
>
> ---
>
> **A**
>
> **Position: Full-time EFL instructor**
>
> **Requirements**: A successful applicant will have a university degree in linguistics and not less than three years of experience in teaching English for Specific Purposes, Business and Correspondence, and Academic English.
>
> **Compensation**: We offer a generous local salary and free accommodation, and will cover 50% of the cost of the DLTC (Diploma in Language Teaching Course) for those who have worked with us for at least one year. Our experienced teacher trainer will provide you with professional guidance, support and advice. Those who are interested in the position should email their CVs to recruitment@xyzschool.com.

B

Position: Full-time primary school teachers wanted

We are the largest primary school in the area currently offering three positions to candidates with a university degree. All candidates will be interviewed for assessment purposes by our team of psychologists.

Compensation: We offer a generous local salary and free accommodation, and will reimburse your travel expenses to and from the city at the end of the contract. Please send your CV and cover letter to recruitment@abcschool.com.

C

Position: Part-time sales representative

One of the largest language schools in the city is looking for an experienced part-time sales representative. An ideal candidate will be able to establish effective communication with our existing and potential clients, and promote our courses and services.

Compensation: The school will cover all the travel expenses incurred as well as the cost of food and accommodation. The successful candidate will receive a base salary of 1,000 Euros a month, plus generous sales commissions. Please send a detailed CV to recruitment@xyzchool.com

Questions that ask you to locate information in paragraphs focus on details within a text and can include opinions, discoveries, theories, and so on. These details may have to be matched, for example, to the names of people in the text. The numbered items are not necessarily in the order in which they appear in the text. Sometimes there are more options than questions, and you must choose a different option for each question. Sometimes there are more questions than options, and you will see the instruction: '*NB You may use any letter more than once.*' The words in the questions or in the box may be paraphrases of words in the passage.

Example 2: Matching

Questions 1 – 5

Reading Passage 1 has ten paragraphs, **A – J**.

Which paragraph contains the following information?

Write the correct letter, **A – J**, next to Questions 1 – 5.

1	The location of the first cinema	....
2	How cinema started to focus on stories	....
3	The speed with which cinema has evolved	....
4	How cinema teaches us about other cultures	....
5	The attraction of actors in films	....

You may be asked to choose suitable headings for some paragraphs or sections of the passage, which will be labelled alphabetically (**A**, **B**, **C**, etc.). For each paragraph a different heading must be chosen (example provided on next page). When matching paragraph headings, you need to choose the heading that best summarises the main idea of the paragraph. When this task is used, it is often the first task for a particular passage, and the headings are given before the passage. There are always more headings than paragraphs.

EXAMPLE 3: MATCHING

Questions 14 – 20

*Reading Passage 2 has seven paragraphs, **A – G**.*

Choose the most suitable heading for each paragraph from the list of headings below.

*Write the correct number, **i – xi**, next to Questions 14 – 20.*

List of headings	
i	A lively social life
ii	A low-fat diet
iii	Drinking coffee
iv	Getting moving
v	Lack of bright light
vi	Low self-esteem
vii	Self-indulgence
viii	Substance abuse
ix	The wrong genes
x	Too much sun
xi	Violence on TV

14	Paragraph **A**	....
15	Paragraph **B**	....
16	Paragraph **C**	....
17	Paragraph **D**	....
18	Paragraph **E**	....
19	Paragraph **F**	....
20	Paragraph **G**	....

TRUE / FALSE / NOT GIVEN QUESTIONS

These questions focus on factual information. They ask you to read statements and compare them to the information given in the passage. You need to decide whether the statement agrees with or contradicts the information in the passage, or whether there is no information about the statement. The questions follow the order of information in the passage. The answers follow this order, but they may be grouped together in one part of the passage or spread across the passage.

If the statement relates to information given in the passage, but the passage does not actually agree or disagree with the statement, you need to select 'Not Given'. If you cannot find the relevant part of the passage, it probably means that the statement is Not Given. If you cannot find the answer to one question, you should leave it and come back to it later. You should remember that you must base their answer on what is in the passage, not on your own knowledge or what you think is likely to be true.

EXAMPLE: TRUE / FALSE / NOT GIVEN QUESTIONS

Questions 10 – 13

Do the following statements agree with the information given in the passage? Next to Questions 10 – 13 write

TRUE	*if the statement agrees with the information*
FALSE	*if the statement contradicts the information*
NOT GIVEN	*if there is no information on this*

10   Wolves in the National Park are a protected species.   ....

11   Some people have exaggerated the danger of wolves to man.   ....

12   Some scientists claim that certain animals are more intelligent than humans.   ....

13   The fear of people may be passed down in the genes of certain animals.   ....

YES / NO / NOT GIVEN

You need to decide whether the statement agrees with or contradicts the writer's views or claims, or whether there is no information relating to the statement in the passage. This task is different from True / False / Not given, which tests your understanding of factual information. However, the approach to the two question types is the same. Many passages include the writer's opinion (views or claims) on a topic as well as providing factual information.

Once you have located the relevant section, you should read it more carefully to decide if the writer agrees, disagrees or does not state an opinion. If you cannot find an answer in the passage, it is possible that the text has no information about this question, and therefore the answer to this question is 'Not Given'. If all parts of the statement agree with the writer's opinion in the text, you should choose 'Yes'. If all or some parts of the statement contradict the writer's opinion, you should answer 'No'.

EXAMPLE: YES / NO / NOT GIVEN

Questions 15 – 20

Do the following statements agree with the views of the writer in the passage? Next to Questions 15 – 20 write

YES	if the statement agrees with the views of the writer
NO	if the statement contradicts the view of the writer
NOT GIVEN	if it is impossible to say what the writer thinks about this

15   An increase in the rate of animal extinctions is likely to have negative ecological consequences. ....

16   More animal species are disappearing than are coming into existence. ....

17   Most animal extinctions are due to natural causes. ....

18   Most efforts to contain animal extinctions have so far been failures. ....

19   Most animal conservation projects are too expensive. ....

20   Working on the programme was a generally positive experience. ....

CLASSIFICATION

In classification tasks, you will see a list of categories and a number of statements. You need to match the statements with the correct categories according to the passage. The statements will be paraphrased—they will have the same meaning as the information in the text, but they may be worded differently. The categories, usually three or more, are all of the same type, for example, periods of time, countries or opinions. The categories will be listed in a logical order, for example, alphabetically. They might not match the order in which they appear in the text. Sometimes the number of categories is the same as the number of statements, but not always. You should skim the passage to decide which section of the passage each category refers to and then scan the sections of the passages you identified to find the ideas that have the same meaning.

EXAMPLE: CLASSIFICATION

Questions 7 – 11

Which countries do the following statements refer to?

Choose your answers from the box and write the correct letters next to Questions 7 – 11.

AU	Australia
CA	Canada
NZ	New Zealand
UK	United Kingdom

7 Some universities are famous for courses in economics. ....

8 Learner autonomy is a priority. ....

9 Institutions offer generous discounts to foreign students. ....

10 It is not a very expensive place to live in. ....

11 Institutions offer an enormous variety of courses and programmes. ....

READING MODULE STRATEGIES

To achieve the best results in the Reading module, you should use a combination of strategies simultaneously. Below are several strategies and tips that will help you with this part of the IELTS exam.

ESSENTIAL READING COMPREHENSION SKILLS

The following reading comprehension tactics are always effective and important to use during the Academic or General Training Reading Modules of the IELTS.

Skimming and Scanning

We use skimming and scanning skills on a regular basis in everyday life. Skimming (reading for general ideas) might be used to decide if a long article will be useful for a research project, or for quickly gathering key information from a report in preparation for a meeting. Scanning (reading for specific information) might be used to find a departure time on a bus timetable or to find out when a movie is playing from a schedule.

Both skimming and scanning involve reading a text quickly, so they are important skills to use on the IELTS exam. However, as you can see, they are used for different goals. Skimming should be used during the IELTS when you need to quickly read for just the main idea of a text, without thinking about specific details. It involves selective reading of the most important parts of the text to find out how the text is organised and get the general idea of what the text is about. Scanning should be used when you need to read to find specific pieces of information such as names, dates and facts.

Identifying Main Ideas and Details

Texts are divided into paragraphs to make them easier to read. A text is usually organised in the following way:

- Introduction: theme, statement and objective
- Paragraph 2: topic, supporting point or details
- Paragraph 3: topic, supporting point or details
- Conclusion: summary and restatement of main idea

In the introduction, the writer usually outlines what he or she is going to write about and the main issues to be raised. Each paragraph usually deals with one key issue, which is stated in a topic sentence and possibly summarised in the last sentence of the paragraph. Supporting details are used to develop and explain the main idea of the paragraph.

EXAMPLE OF PARAGRAPH ORGANISATION

[Introduction]

Article theme: What are the connections between psychological and physical well-being?

[Paragraph]

Topic and main idea: Regular exercise makes people happier.

Detail: endorphins

Extract:

[Introduction]

Open almost any newspaper or magazine these days and we find doctors and scientists telling us that being healthy directly affects our psychological well-being. But exactly what do the experts say about what makes us feel good?

[Paragraph]

Regular exercise is obviously a good way to keep healthy and fit, but scientists now think that exercise improves our psychological health by releasing chemicals called 'endorphins' into the brain. Endorphins have been shown to elevate feelings of happiness and well-being. Some scientists claim that exercise can be as useful a treatment for depression as psychotherapy, and that by lifting our mood, it can help us feel more positive about ourselves and our lives. According to some doctors, something as seemingly simple as a daily ten-minute walk can greatly improve our quality of life.

Understanding Opinion

An opinion is a personal belief which may or may not be true. It is different from a fact, which is a statement known to be true or based on generally accepted evidence. In texts, opinions are usually introduced by phrases such as:

- Professor Jones argues that …
- Several experts claim that …
- Some people say that …
- It is a commonly held belief that …
- In Harriet's view, …
- Many scientists suspect that …

Facts, on the other hand, might be introduced by phrases such as:

- According to the latest statistics, …
- Scientists have discovered …
- Research findings confirm that …
- As has been frequently demonstrated, …

When answering questions related to the writer's opinion, you should be careful not to allow your own opinions to interfere with your choice of answer. You should remember that you are looking for the writer's idea, not your own.

GENERAL STRATEGIES FOR THE READING MODULE

The following strategies are always effective. It is important to use them for all Reading module question types.

Strategy 1: Make notes.

You are allowed to make notes on IELTS question booklets, and IELTS examiners will never look at these notes. During the examination, you can make notes, underline, or draw arrows and symbols on the reading question booklet to help yourself understand the text better and find answers faster. This might help you avoid having to read the same portions of the text again to refresh your memory.

Strategy 2: Try to predict what you are going to read about.

Before you read a text in the IELTS Reading module, try to guess what the topics of that passage will be. One way to do this is to use the information in the title, any subheadings and the introduction.

Strategy 3: Build a mental map of the passage as you are skimming it.

Reading a text for the first time can be disorientating—you may find it difficult to find your way around. A useful technique to help you 'navigate' a text is to build a mental map. Identify the topic or purpose of each paragraph in the passage. Make notes (a couple of words) about the main idea or purpose of paragraphs and sections next to them to help you. Knowing what the paragraphs are about will help you find answers faster.

Strategy 4: Identify the type of text you are reading.

For example, identify whether it is about a problem and a solution, or a chronological account of something, or whether it discusses positive and negative points regarding a certain topic, and so on. This can be done by quickly skimming the text and looking at the title, introduction and paragraph openings. These will give you the clues needed to identify the main ideas, topics and organisation of the text.

Strategy 5: Study the keywords.

To locate the parts of the text where the answers might be, carefully study the keywords in the questions and then scan the text for these or synonymous and parallel expressions. Using your mental map of the text should help you do this.

Strategy 6: Skim actively.

When you skim a text, try not to worry about words you do not understand. Instead, try to get an overall impression of the text, making sure you read the first sentence of each paragraph. These will give you an overview of the text. Remember that sometimes two different task types may focus on the same part of the text. However, you will not be tested on exactly the same information.

Strategy 7: Make intelligent guesses.

To read effectively, you need to make intelligent guesses about the meaning of words you do not know, if they seem important in the context. Try to work out the meaning from the surrounding words and sentences, and think of other words that might fit the context.

Strategy 8: Don't lose track of time.

You must enter your answers on the separate answer sheet during the 60 minutes allowed for the module. You can either write your answers directly on the answer sheet as you go through the test or transfer them later, making sure you leave at least 10 minutes for this.

If you cannot figure out an answer, go on to the next question. Some questions in the reading test might be easier than other questions, so it is a good idea to save as much time as possible by dealing quickly with the easier questions. Before you move on to other questions, do not forget to mark the difficult one with some sort of symbol, like a question mark, so that you can easily find it later, if you still have time for this.

SPECIFIC STRATEGIES FOR READING MODULE QUESTION TYPES

The following strategies refer to skills that are always important to use for certain Reading module question types.

COMPLETION TASKS

- You should only include the words essential to answering the question correctly. Correct answers can contain fewer than the maximum number of words stated in the instructions.

- In completion tasks with words taken directly from the text, you should try to predict the type of answer you are looking for. Next, skim the section you have identified and look for synonyms and paraphrases. Think about both the meaning and the grammar and remember to use the exact word(s) from the passage; in this type of task, you must not change the form of the words you add in any way.

- In completion tasks with options given in a box, you should read the options carefully. It is likely that more than one option could complete the sentence, as options will often have the same grammatical structure. You should therefore focus more on the meaning of the sentence than on grammar. You need to consider all the options in the box. When you have finished, you need to check that you have not used the same option twice.

MULTIPLE-CHOICE TASKS

- First try to eliminate the options that seem logically wrong. Eliminate options by putting a cross beside them when you are sure they are wrong. Remember, in some cases an option may be true, but does not answer the question.

- Check that the answer you choose is not only correct according to the passage, but also gives an appropriate reason or explanation to answer the question or complete the sentence. When you think you have found the correct answer to a multiple-choice question, remember to check that the three other options are definitely wrong.

MATCHING TASKS

- When matching pictures to sections of text, try to think of different words to describe what is in each picture and look for keywords in the texts. Match the ones you are sure about first and the more difficult ones second. When matching statements, try to identify keywords in the statements and look for synonyms or paraphrases of these keywords in the text(s).

- You should skim the passage to build a 'mental map' of the text by noting the main idea of each paragraph. It is good idea to match as many headings as you can without reading the passage again, and cross off the headings you have used, including the example.

- Beside each paragraph you should write the number of all the options that might be suitable. Then make sure each possible option fits the meaning of the whole paragraph and does not simply use some of the same words.

READING MODULE PRACTICE SECTIONS

In this section, you will find full-length practice sections for the Academic and General Training Reading modules. You can write your answers and make notes the on pages in the book.

GO ON TO THE NEXT PAGE

8-27
47

ACADEMIC READING PASSAGE 1

You should spend about 20 minutes on Questions 1 – 15, which are based on Reading Passage 1 below.

A Global Warning

A *The Stern Review Report on The Economics of Climate Change*, published in 2006, the same year as Al Gore's highly-acclaimed film and book, *An Inconvenient Truth*, made it clear that governments need to take the issue of global warming very seriously indeed. The Stern Review examined the issue of climate change from an economic perspective, looking at what it would cost the government to take appropriate action, and what it would cost if appropriate action were not taken. The report also highlighted a number of catastrophes that would occur if urgent measures were not taken to stop the carbon dioxide production that is heating up the planet. The report indicates that in the last 200 years, average temperatures on the planet have increased by less than one degree Celsius; however, if we do not control the rising carbon dioxide levels over the next 100 years, a rise of up to five degrees Celsius can be expected. This will have an enormous impact on global economic growth and will cause many potentially disastrous changes, including the following:

B Melting glaciers—Beginning in the Andes, and then extending to the huge glaciers of the Himalayas, the ice will begin to disappear, threatening the water supply of billions of people. Sea levels will also rise, flooding huge areas of the world, including cities such as London and Tokyo.

C Melting ice sheets—Not only will glaciers melt, but as the planet warms up, the huge Antarctic Ice Sheets and the floating sea ice of the Arctic will begin to melt, again resulting in catastrophic rises in sea levels. It is estimated that Arctic summers will be ice-free within 10 years, and the landscapes of the Antarctic will change beyond recognition by 2050. The vast ice plains of Greenland are also under threat.

D The acidity resulting from the huge amounts of CO_2 that the oceans will absorb will lead to the extinction of hundreds of species as marine ecosystems are destroyed; this will also threaten the fishing industry as thousands of millions of fish die off. This in turn will destroy the livelihood of thousands of fishing communities that depend on already overfished coastal areas.

E Accompanying the floods will be an increasing occurrence of droughts, with a decrease of up to 30% in water availability in Africa, and similar decreases in Australia. This will, of course, result in crop failure and malnutrition the world over. It will also lead to an increase in disease, particularly in tropical regions. Large cities in dry regions will find it increasingly difficult to provide enough water for their populations.

F   Hurricanes, cyclones and tidal waves—Both Al Gore's book and the Stern Review indicate that if global temperatures continue to rise, we can expect a greater number of extreme weather phenomena, of an increased severity. Hurricane Katrina, which devastated the United States in 2005, is cited as just one example of the kind of environmental and economic havoc that will result from unchecked global warming. Typhoons, which often cause extensive flooding, are becoming more frequent and devastating in South East Asia.

G   Up to 50% of animal and plant species on the planet, beginning with those living in fragile environments such as coral reefs, tropical rainforest and alpine tundra, will become extinct. Climate change will eventually affect every ecosystem on the planet as temperatures increase, rainforest is destroyed and sea levels rise, leading to flooding and drought. The impact on ecosystems will be so dramatic that they will never recover from the damage caused by rising temperatures.

H   Does all this sound too depressing even to contemplate? Well, don't despair: if you are optimistic by nature, there are two approaches to tackling the problem of global warming you could take.

I   The first approach is to begin to act locally to do your bit to reduce CO_2 emissions and minimise pollution, at the same time hoping that governments will listen to the recommendations of the Stern Review, which, while recognising the seriousness of the threat, clearly indicates that if action is taken now, the right balance between economic growth and environmental conservation may be achieved. The Report is significant, both in its scope and its depth, and it does offer a positive outcome that allows economic growth to continue—so perhaps this will convince governments to take the action necessary to save the planet from environmental and economic disaster.

J   The second approach you could take, if you wish to remain optimistic, is to disregard the warnings of Al Gore, the Stern Review team and other like-minded harbingers of doom, and instead opt for the much more positive and less dramatic stance taken by a very different group of scientists and economists. With its nominal leader the Danish economist, Bjorn Lomborg, the Omgivelse group believes that many of the predictions of the environmentalists are hugely exaggerated. Like Stern, Lomborg takes a pragmatic economic approach to the environmental situation and argues for investment in environmental research and development, rather than 'quick-fix' measures that would not, he claims, solve the problem. With significantly less investment than that recommended in the Kyoto Accord or by the Stern Review Report, Lomborg believes the planet can be saved.

Questions 1 – 3

Complete the summary below.

Choose **NO MORE THAN THREE WORDS** *from the passage for each answer.*

The Stern Review Report emphasised the ...**1**... to assess seriously the problem of global warming from ...**2**... point of view. It also focused on a number of environmental ...**3**... that would happen if governments do not act to prevent climate change.

1 .... 2 .... 3 ....

Questions 4 – 12

*Reading Passage 1 has ten paragraphs, **A – J**.*

*Choose the most suitable heading, **i – xiii**, for each paragraph from the list of the headings below.*

*Write the correct numbers, **i – xiii**, next to Questions 4 – 12.*

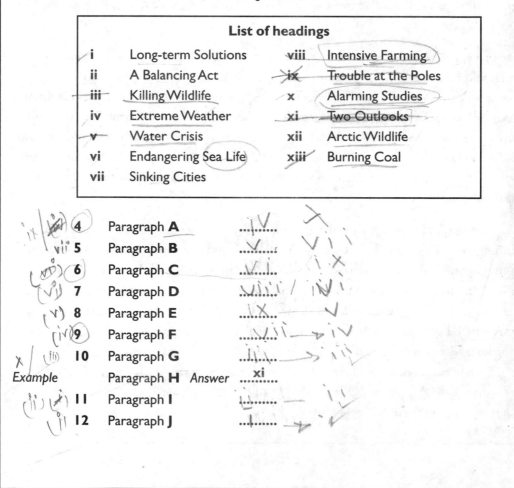

List of headings		
i	Long-term Solutions	viii Intensive Farming
ii	A Balancing Act	ix Trouble at the Poles
iii	Killing Wildlife	x Alarming Studies
iv	Extreme Weather	xi Two Outlooks
v	Water Crisis	xii Arctic Wildlife
vi	Endangering Sea Life	xiii Burning Coal
vii	Sinking Cities	

4 Paragraph **A** ....
5 Paragraph **B** ....
6 Paragraph **C** ....
7 Paragraph **D** ....
8 Paragraph **E** ....
9 Paragraph **F** ....
10 Paragraph **G** ....
Example Paragraph **H** *Answer* ...xi...
11 Paragraph **I** ....
12 Paragraph **J** ....

Questions 13 – 15

Complete each of the following statements, 1 – 3, with the best ending, **A – H**, from the list of endings below.

Write the correct letters, **A – H**, next to Questions 13 –15.

Example   Answer
Lomborg believes that we can ....**E**...... .

1 The Stern Review points out that it is not too late ....

2 More optimistic commentators like Bjorn Lomborg believe that politicians and scientists need ....

3 Bjorn Lomborg argues that short-term measures will not help ....

List of endings

A   to sign international environmental treaties.

B   to strike the balance between economy and environment.

C   to take personal responsibility for reducing CO_2 emissions.

D   to stop exaggerating the issue.

E   save the planet.

F   to find a solution to the problem.

G   the issue of global warming.

H   the problem of water pollution.

---

2 ⁴⁄₂₅

ACADEMIC READING PASSAGE 2

You should spend about 20 minutes on Questions 1 – 15, which are based on Reading Passage 2 below.

Cure-all Pills: Myth or Reality?

Browse the shelves of any health food shop or pharmacy and you'll find dozens of dietary supplements—vitamins, antioxidants, minerals—along with a seemingly endless range of homeopathic remedies. There is always something new, some 'miracle ingredient' offering the promise of a longer, healthier, happier life. There are extracts of every kind of fruit and vegetable you can imagine—tomato, celery, carrot, papaya and cranberry—along with green tea potion, red wine extract and vitamins A–K in every colour and form. And all of these supplements claim to assist us in the constant battle against ageing, cancer, cardio-vascular disease, and a cornucopia of other afflictions. However, recent research may show it is all too good to be true.

So how real are these claims? Vitamin tablets have been around forever, but antioxidants are the latest miracle cure; the question is, do they work? If the hype is true, then what antioxidants do is work to neutralise the free radicals in our bodies and later excrete them. Free radicals are atoms or molecules that have at least one unpaired electron and are therefore unstable and highly reactive. In animal tissue they are believed to accelerate the progression of cardio-vascular and age-related diseases, such as dementia and cancer. Antioxidants in fresh fruit and vegetables have been shown to combine with free radicals and neutralise them, preventing the oxidation which may lead to disease.

'An apple a day keeps the doctor away'—if eaten alongside four other portions of fresh fruit and vegetables! It is clear that those who eat more fruit and vegetables—and the recommended daily intake is at least five portions—are less prone to disease and live longer, healthier lives. Over the last 20–30 years, scientists have worked to isolate the active ingredients in fruit and vegetables—believed to be the antioxidants—and have conducted controlled tests of antioxidants, which revealed that they do indeed appear to have the ability to halt some of the chemical processes that cause disease. Thus the multimillion dollar industry of bottled antioxidants to supplement the diets of the busy and the stressed was born.

Antioxidants were first cast into doubt during a major clinical trial in the US, in which a very common antioxidant, beta-carotene, also known as pro-vitamin A (found in yellow and green vegetables, milk and fish), was being tested for its efficacy against lung cancer in high-risk subjects. To the surprise and concern of the scientists conducting the experiment, those individuals taking the supplement—intended to reduce the risk of cancer—were at a significantly higher risk of developing lung cancer. This startling discovery led to the abandonment of the trials mid-way through the experimental process.

Since this experiment in the mid-90s, other studies have similarly indicated that antioxidants and vitamin supplements are of dubious health value at best, and may possibly be harmful. It seems that even common vitamin supplements such as vitamin C may, in large doses, actually exacerbate the risk of cardio-vascular disease or cancer.

As a result of these recent alarming studies, the US Food and Drug Administration (FDA) and its European equivalent, the European Medicine Agency (EMEA), have taken the decision to prohibit the production and sale of a number of the higher-dose supplements currently on the market.

Another aspect of the increasingly complex picture to take into account is that recent research findings have also called into question some previously held beliefs concerning free radicals. It is possible, some scientists believe, that free radicals actually play a role in preventing disease. Professor Jennifer Horton at the University of West Wyoming is one of a number of scientists who has found that in small amounts, the free radicals may help stimulate the antioxidant systems in our bodies. It is also becoming apparent that free radicals may play a fundamental role in the fight against disease; recent research in the UK suggests that they kill off harmful bacteria and even cancerous cells.

Clearly, then, the use of bottled supplements with your diet is a practice to approach warily; and it is essential to keep abreast of new developments in research. Ironically, those health-conscious individuals who already eat large quantities of fresh fruit and vegetables, whose diet does not include junk food and who get plenty of regular exercise and have less need for dietary supplements tend to be the ones who are most likely to use them.

abreast
warily

Questions 1 – 4

*Choose the correct letters, **A – D**.*

1   When introducing his discussion on antioxidant diet supplements, the writer notes
    that

    A   most supplements sold in pharmacies or health food shops have at least
    some proven health benefits.

    B   very few diet supplements are regulated by government health agencies.

    C   there is evidence that some dietary supplements can be bad for your
    health.

    D   only a few products offer real protection against ageing, heart disease and
    cancer.

2   In the fourth paragraph, the writer's main point is that

    A   very high doses of antioxidant supplements can harm the liver.

    B   US doctors prescribe pro-vitamin A to patients..

    C   the clinical trials did not produce any conclusive results.

    D   antioxidant supplements can increase the risk of some cancers.

3   According to the writer,

    A   recent studies have confirmed the benefits of antioxidants.

    B   vitamin C supplements help to decrease the risk of heart disease.

    C   the European Union endorses some higher-dose vitamin supplements.

    D   some governments have banned a number of higher-dose vitamin
    supplements.

4   The writer suggests that

    A   it is better to take vitamin supplements than not to take them.

    B   it is important to be well-informed about vitamin supplements before
    taking them.

    C   people who exercise regularly should supplement their diets with vitamins.

    D   vitamins and antioxidants are less effective when consumed as food.

Questions 5 – 10

Do the following statements agree with the information in Reading Passage 2?
Next to Questions 5 – 10, write

TRUE	if the statement is true according to the passage
FALSE	if the statement is false according to the passage
NOT GIVEN	if the information is not given in the passage

5   Vitamin supplements bought from health food shops can differ from
    those available at pharmacies.   ....

6   Antioxidants eliminate free radicals from the body.   ....

7   After the release of Professor Horton's study, the number of people
    taking vitamin supplements declined.   ....

8   The findings of studies into the effect of pro-vitamin A resulted in
    some US drug companies going on trial.   ....

9   The FDA and the EMEA have jointly funded research into the safety
    of certain higher-dose vitamin supplements.   ....

10 Recent research suggests that small amounts of free radicals can
    help prevent disease.   ....

Questions 11 – 15

Complete the sentences below with words taken from Reading Passage 2.

Use NO MORE THAN THREE WORDS for each answer.

1   Professor Jennifer Horton says that small amounts of 11 _____ may be beneficial for our bodies.

2   Some studies have indicated that vitamin supplements can be 12 _____

3   Free radicals may have an important function in 13 _____

4   14 _____ people tend to be the ones who use bottled supplements.

5   You should 15 _____ the use of bottled vitamin supplements with caution.

2⁴45

ACADEMIC READING PASSAGE 3

You should spend about 20 minutes on Questions 1 – 15, which are based on Reading Passage 3 below.

Water and Chips Break New Ground

Computers have been shrinking ever since their conception almost two centuries ago, and the trend is set to continue with the latest developments in microchip manufacturing.

The earliest prototype of a mechanical computer was called the Difference Engine, and was invented by an eccentric Victorian called Charles Babbage. It weighed over 15 tons and had 26,000 parts. Colossus, the first electronic computer, did not appear until the end of WWII, and with its 1,500 vacuum tubes was even more complex and much heavier than its mechanical predecessor.

It was only when the silicon-based microchip was invented in the early 1950s that computers started to become more compact. The first microchip computers were very complex and had more than 100,000 transistors, or electronic switches; however, they were still rather bulky and measured several metres across. Nowadays microchips are measured in nanometres (nm)—that is, in billionths of a metre—and the search for even smaller microchips continues as scientists work on new methods of microchip production.

Today, most microchips are shaped by a process called lithographic etching, which uses ultraviolet (UV) light. A beam of UV light with a wavelength of only 193 nm is projected through a lens on to an etching mask, a micro device with slits, or long narrow cuts. When the UV light hits the surface of silicon chips, it removes microscopic layers of silicon to create patterns for the microchip's circuits. Microchips with features as small as 65 nm can be created with this wavelength.

However, lithographic etching is unable to make chips much smaller than 65 nm due to the fundamental properties of light. If the slit in the mask were made narrower, the air and nitrogen used in the space between the lens and the etching mask would diffuse the light, causing a blurred image. This means that 193-nm UV light cannot be used to produce microchips with features smaller than 65 nm. Manufacturers know that they need to go even smaller for the technological demands of this century, and they are looking for new methods of making microchips.

One approach to solving the problem is to use microscopic mirrors to focus X-rays rather than ultraviolet light. X-rays with a wavelength of less than 25 nm can be created, allowing engineers to make components smaller than 15 nm. The process is known as X-ray lithography etching. However, this technology is extremely expensive, so manufacturers are continuing to search for a cheaper alternative.

A technology called immersion lithography might be the solution. Although liquids are not commonly associated with computers, a tiny drop of water may be all it takes to make microprocessors smaller and more powerful. Intel and IBM, who made the first microprocessors, have recently developed a unique method of microchip production, which uses water droplets to enable manufacturers to shrink the chips—and at a reasonable price! The new microchip is produced by using a drop of water to narrow the gap between the light source and the etching mask, and shorten the wavelength of the UV light to less than 34 nm. This process can be used to manufacture microchips as small as 45 nm, or possibly even smaller.

Initially, engineers feared that air bubbles and other contaminants in water drops would distort the light and ruin the microchip etching process, and the first experiments proved these fears to be well-founded. The problem was overcome by using high-purity water, free of air and other substances. Scientists are also experimenting with liquids other than water—denser liquids such as hydrofluoric acid—which may allow the wavelength to be shrunk still further, thus producing even smaller chips.

IBM have already successfully implemented immersion lithography on some of their production lines and created a fully-functioning microprocessor. IBM also claim that they are able to produce microchips with very few defects.

Although immersion lithography is very new, it is highly promising as it will make the production of 45 nm and 32 nm chips commercially viable. It is a significant milestone in chip manufacturing and will help to bring the costs of the chip down without fundamentally changing the microchip production processes.

In the near future, the ground-breaking technology of immersion lithography will enable computer manufacturers to make powerful microchips that will be used in electronic devices smaller than a coin. This will open up new opportunities in the ever-shrinking world of digital technology.

Questions 1 – 5

Do the following statements agree with the information given in the reading passage?
Next to Questions 1-5, write

TRUE	*if the statement is true according to the passage*
FALSE	*if the statement is false according to the passage*
NOT GIVEN	*if the information is not given in the passage*

1   The first electronic computer weighed more than the first mechanical prototype. ....

2   Computers started to shrink with the invention of the microchip. ....

3   In early 1950s engineers used ultraviolet rays to build the first microchip. ....

4   X-ray lithography is an inexpensive alternative technology to lithographic etching. ....

5   Immersion lithography has enabled microchip manufacturers to produce higher quality computer chips. ....

Questions 6 – 9

Label the diagram below.

Choose NO MORE THAN TWO WORDS from the passage for each answer.

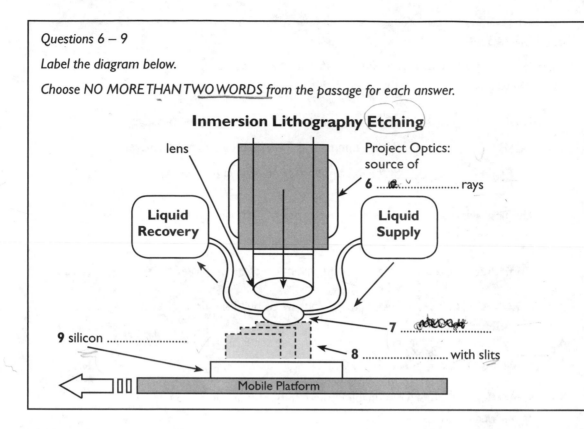

Inmersion Lithography Etching

lens

Project Optics:
source of

6 .... rays

Liquid Recovery

Liquid Supply

7 ....

9 silicon ....

8 .... with slits

Mobile Platform

Questions 10 – 15

Complete the table below.

Choose NO MORE THAN THREE WORDS from the passage for each answer.

Method	Light used	Wavelength	Material used to condense light
Lithography	Ultraviolet	193 nm	air or 13 ....
Immersion Lithography	10	11	14 ....
X-ray Lithography	X-rays	12	15 ....

12 20

GENERAL READING PASSAGE 1

You should spend about 20 minutes on Questions 1 – 15, which are based on Reading Passage 1 below.

The Dream Hotel

A I don't want to get your hopes up, but I think I may have discovered the perfect hotel! Naturally, it's in one of the world's most amazing cities—Barcelona, home to Gaudí, Picasso, Miró and a football club with worshippers from London to Beijing. The Gracia, which opened last year in a building designed by Antoni Gaudí in 1870, was spectacularly renovated by the young architectural team Alonso i Pujol. Situated on the aptly-named Passeig de Gracia (*gracia* means grace or gracious), you couldn't ask for a better location—all the shopping, tapas, architectural wonders and haute cuisine you could ask for within a stone's throw of the Gracia's beautifully renovated modernist lobby. The rooms have been designed with typical Barcelona flair, the service is impeccable, and the food is, quite simply, divine.

B The Güell Bar is the place to meet for a drink and tapas in Barcelona. You may find it just a little too popular if your tastes run to a quiet drink in a peaceful little corner. The Güell is not quiet—it's buzzing, it's elegant, it's sophisticated and it's beautifully designed and furnished. But there are no quiet corners! There is a terrace from which to view the sunset over the city as you sip your cocktails, and a team of bar-staff who can make you the best version of any drink you've ever tried. And all against the backdrop of Gaudí's twisting, flowing columns and doorways.

C After a big day out—shopping, beach, drinks on the seafront, dinner in the hotel restaurant— you'll be grateful for the luxury on offer in your room or suite. Each room has all the sophistication you would expect, with elegance almost breathtaking in its simplicity—soft whites and neutral tones, bathrooms with hot tub and personal sauna, king-sized beds—while offering all the modern comforts and technologies you could possibly wish for. And room service runs not only to champagne and sushi; you can also request a Thai or Shiatsu massage in your room, a beauty treatment or translation services.

D Spain is home to 30 of the world's top 50 chefs—and at The Gracia this is brought home with every mouthful. There are two restaurants: The Atrium, where breakfast and lunch are served, and Gracia, open for lunch and dinner. Both are beautiful places to eat. The Atrium is an air-conditioned tropical paradise, with lush ferns, orchids and waterfalls providing the backdrop to a wonderful breakfast. You can select the buffet—a rich offering of fruit platters, freshly-baked pastries, cold meats and cheeses—or the à la carte breakfast, should you fancy Eggs Benedict, sushi or a banana lassi. Gracia provides a totally different dining context—European sophistication in an atmosphere of understated luxury. And the food … I can still taste the foam of wild mushrooms, cava and herbs, or the mille-feuille of gambas, lemon-grass and coriander. And all accompanied by the world-renowned wines and cavas of the region.

E   I can't finish without making further mention of the amazing staff of this hotel. They were flawless—multi-lingual, attentive (but never intrusive), with a solution to every problem I could come up with! There was always someone to open a door, serve a drink, answer a phone or help with an enquiry—but afterwards, you couldn´t actually remember the encounter, it was so unobtrusive.

F   Not as much as you might think—for a hotel of this quality and location. A double will set you back 230€–280€, with all taxes and charges included. But if you can afford a bit more, go for one of the four penthouse suites—the height of luxury, very spacious and with incredible views of the city. At 400€ the experience does not come cheap, but it's well worth it.

G   Get online and check out Gracia's website on www.gracia.com; you can book through the website too. Or call (34) 93 467 5896.

Questions 1 – 6

Reading Passage 1 has seven paragraphs, **A – G**.

Choose the most suitable heading, **i – ix**, for each paragraph from the list of headings below.

Write the correct numbers, **i – ix**, next to Questions 1 – 6.

List of headings

i	The Location	vi	Getting There
ii	How to Book	vii	Wining and Dining
iii	Sightseeing	viii	And Finally …
iv	What It'll Cost You	ix	Drinks
v	The Interior		

1	Paragraph **A**		………..
2	Paragraph **B**		………..
Example	Paragraph **C**	Answer	…..v…..
3	Paragraph **D**		………..
4	Paragraph **E**		………..
5	Paragraph **F**		………..
6	Paragraph **G**		………..

Questions 7 – 12

Do the following statements agree with the information given in the reading passage?
Next to Questions 7 – 12, write

TRUE	*if the statement is true according to the passage*
FALSE	*if the statement is false according to the passage*
NOT GIVEN	*if the information is not given in the passage*

7   The Güell bar is located in a quiet place.   ....

8   Guests can order champagne to be brought to their room.   ....

9   The Atrium and Gracia restaurants are very similar.   ....

10   The hotel staff are fluent in several languages.   ....

11   You must use a credit card to book a room at the hotel.   ....

12   You can reserve a room online.   ....

Questions 13 – 15

Using NO MORE THAN THREE WORDS, answer the following questions.

13   When was the hotel building designed?   ....

14   Where can you watch the sunset?   ....

15   How much does a night in a penthouse suite cost?   ....

12ʰ40

GENERAL READING PASSAGE 2

You should spend about 20 minutes on Questions 1 – 16, which are based on Reading Passage 2 below.

Digital Photography Courses

The Department of Media Design offers digital photography courses to all first-year students. The courses are offered at two levels.

Digital Photography Level 1 is a 20-hour course aimed at students with little or no experience of digital photography, and is designed to teach the essentials of digital photography to people at beginner level. Course participants will learn about digital camera settings and modes, image file types and sizes, and image manipulating software.

Digital Photography Level 2 is a 30-hour course aimed at people with some experience and knowledge of the subject. Participants who wish to enrol on the course should be familiar with digital camera settings and modes and Adobe Photoshop© software. The course covers advanced camera settings which include exposure, flash compensation and shutter speeds. Participants will also learn advanced image processing techniques and principles of photo composition and photo image printing. At the end of the course, participants are expected to submit a project portfolio.

Qualified trainers, graduates of the Media Studies Department who are all experienced professional photographers working full-time in the media industry, will be delivering the course to four groups of maximum 10 participants each.

How to enrol

You can leave the application form at the main desk at Lincoln Library or fill it in online at www.digiphoto.uk.edu/application. Tuition is free and applications are open to all first-year students; second- and third-year students enrolled in Marketing or Web Design courses can also apply. To qualify for a place, you must attach a photocopy of your student ID card to the application.

Participants are expected to use their own digital cameras, but each participant will have access to a university computer. The courses run every month three times a week for four weeks, starting the second week of Semester One. The classes are held in the Lincoln Library Learning Centre.

University students who successfully complete the course can earn five credits towards their degree if the course is part of their degree programme. Students who take the course outside the required degree programme can take a final test and will be awarded a certificate. Participants wishing to take the test will be charged £10 for the certificate at the beginning of the course.

For more information, please visit www.digiphoto.uk.edu/courses or call the Lincoln Library Main Desk 3498876 Ext. 401.

Questions 1 – 3

*Choose the correct letter, **A – D**, from the options below.*

1   The course is aimed at

    A   only Media Design students.

    B   all second-year students.

    C   all first-year students.

    D   only second- and third-year students.

2   Students who wish to enrol in the Level 2 course need to

    A   have their own computer.

    B   have some knowledge of digital cameras.

    C   know the principles of photo composition.

    D   show a project portfolio.

3   All course trainers

    A   teach Media Studies at the university.

    B   studied at the university.

    C   have taught the courses before.

    D   work full-time at the university.

Questions 4 – 8

Do the following statements agree with the information given in the reading passage?
Next to Questions 4 – 8, write

TRUE	*if the statement is true according to the passage*
FALSE	*if the statement is false according to the passage*
NOT GIVEN	*if the information is not given in the passage*

4 You can fill in the application electronically. ....

5 Applicants must buy a course book. ....

6 Digital cameras and computers will be provided by the university. ....

7 The courses run only in Semester One. ....

8 Every student who successfully completes the course can earn credits towards his/her degree. ....

Questions 9 – 16

Read the information below and answer Questions 9 – 16.

Blogs: Web Publishing for Everyone

A Since its conception in the early 1970s, the Internet has grown in popularity and is nowadays taken for granted by many of its users. Many sceptics and optimists who saw the dot-com boom of the late 1990s turn sour wrote off the Internet as just another tech fad. The investment banks may have turned their backs on the huge constellations of optical fibre cables, computers and servers that make up the Net as the tech investment boom subsided, but the Internet is now reaching more kinds of people in more kinds of places as consumer demand for Internet connections continues to grow. The Internet has dramatically changed the way people interact with each other and communicate electronically.

B Communication is what the Internet is best at and the main reason that it is so widely used by millions of people. Email is still the main activity for which people use the Internet, but the Internet is evolving at a breathtaking pace, has changed the way we interact digitally, and has made terms such as 'wiki', 'podcast', and 'online shopping' household words. Words like 'messaging', 'googling 'and 'youtubing' describe what many of us do every day. Blogging is just one of the buzz words, but is still new to many who use the Internet just to email friends and relatives. What, then is a blog, and what is blogging?

C The Internet has made information on any conceivable subject available with just a mouse click, but it is blogging that has enabled millions of individuals to share information freely. In one form or another, technologies that enable one-to-one communication have been around for a while. Blogging has given the individual a one-to-many technological platform which can be used to share ideas online with the world daily by 'logging' them on the Web. Web logging or 'blogging' exploded in popularity in 2003 when over 1,000 blogs were being created every day. A weblog, or blog for short, is basically a journal that is published on the Web.

D The number of blogs has increased dramatically over the last few years, and there are now an estimated 4.6 million blogs on the ten biggest Web publishing sites. Enthusiastic social and political commentators have been sharing ideas and leaving comments on one another's blogs for years; these are now part of a growing 'blogosphere'. Some of the best-known blogs such as 'The Daily Dish' and 'Exactly 2¢ Worth' get around 35,000 hits a day.

E People from all walks of life write and comment on blogs. Recent surveys have shown that blogs are most popular with teenagers, with about half of all blogs published and maintained by under-18s. Some early research suggested that women blog more often than men. However, surveys on some of the most popular blog sites such as 'E Blogger' show that both sexes sign up for blogging accounts in approximately equal numbers.

F   Blogs are a great place to find personal reviews of websites and read independent commentaries on daily news. Unlike newspapers, they offer a more personal perspective and blog visitors can interact by responding to one another's comments and adding them to blog message boards. Blogs are aimed at much smaller audiences than newspapers. Similar-minded people are often the most active contributors who discuss and exchange ideas on special interest blogs.

G   Blogs can take many different forms. Some weblogs are personal diaries, many have links and quotes from other websites, and some are used as a platform to express opinions about world affairs, a hobby or a specialist interest. There are travel blogs, project and educational blogs, and legal blogs—which are often called 'blawgs'. Some forms of blogging have evolved into vlogs where users post short videos, or photoblogs with lots of images.

H   You do not need to be tech-savvy or rich to start publishing on the Web. Setting up a blog is as easy as signing up for an email account. If you think you have something interesting to share with the world of like-minded web readers, all you need is a computer connected to the Internet, an email address and 10-15 minutes of your time. However, what many bloggers find difficult is to build up an audience for their blogs and to find the time, patience and creativity to update the blog and maintain the interest of their blog readers. You can use a search engine to look up blogs on the topics that interest you to see how they work and leave a comment or two.

I   Internet technologies like blogs and wikis may or may not turn out to have long-lasting importance, but blog popularity does not show signs of abating. Blogging has shifted the balance of power in web publishing and given Internet users a tool to voice their opinions, putting them on both the receiving and the giving end of information flow.

Questions 9 – 16

The reading passage has nine paragraphs, **A – I**.

Choose the most suitable heading, **i – ix**, for each paragraph from the list of the headings below.

Write the correct numbers, **i – ix**, next to Questions 9 – 16.

List of headings

i	A Voice for Everyone	vii	Blog Popularity
ii	The Power of the Net	viii	Bloggers
iii	New Tools New Words	ix	Online Banking
iv	Why Read Blogs	x	Types of Blog
v	Blogging Explained	xi	Technical Challenge
vi	Where to Start		

9	Paragraph **A**	....
10	Paragraph **B**	....
11	Paragraph **C**	....
12	Paragraph **D**	....
13	Paragraph **E**	....
14	Paragraph **F**	....
Example	Paragraph **G** *Answer*	....x....
15	Paragraph **H**	....
16	Paragraph **I**	....

GENERAL READING PASSAGE 3

You should spend about 20 minutes on Questions 1 – 15, which are based on Reading Passage 3 below.

Speaking in Many Tongues

Sandra Fisher, 53, speaks 42 languages. As well as her native English and German, she picked up the Italian and Greek spoken by immigrants in her home town of Armidale in New South Wales, Australia; she also quickly learnt the Aboriginal language spoken by the Coorie children at her primary school. When asked how she does it, she really can't explain. 'I just listen for a few minutes, and then I start to speak, and somehow, I just start to see the patterns in my head, I can understand and speak without studying or even thinking very much.'

Basia Dombrowski, 19, is another 'language-learning phenomenon'. Born in a small town in Poland, she is unable to say what her mother tongue is: 'I'm told that my first words came from four different languages,' she says, 'the native dialects of my grandmother who raised me, and of the servant who helped care for me, the Polish my mother spoke and the Yiddish of my father. At first I spoke isolated words from each language, but by 18 months, I was speaking in whole sentences in all four languages, but never mixing them.' As an adult, Basia speaks about 30 languages fluently and is always keen to learn more. 'I guess you could say it's my hobby,' she says in perfect English. 'I don't use the languages I learn in my work as a painter, but I do love to speak to people.'

How do people learn languages? Is it an innate human ability, such as the ability to speak and reason, or is it something that we learn 'from scratch'—a system that we learn, fitting the elements of language into it as we learn them, taking into account the environment in which we find ourselves?

Advocates of the former point of view note that all humans are able to learn their native language in the first four or five years of life, whatever the language, and despite the complexity of the linguistic systems that they need to master. This is because, according to the most famous proponent of this theory, Noam Chomsky, we are all born with a 'language acquisition device' in our brains. What he is saying, effectively, is that language-learning knowledge is 'built in', and that we are hard-wired, as it were, to learn a language from birth.

Cognitive linguists like Elizabeth Bates claim that most important is our interaction with other humans and the social environment, and it is this that helps us learn a language.

Still other researchers, like biolinguists Lenneberg and Piatelli, suggest that we may have a special language-learning gene or genes—and that these genes will determine whether we are poor, average or excellent learners of a foreign language.

Whatever the explanation, one thing we can be sure of is that there are some outstanding language learners who seem to pick up foreign languages with astonishing ease—and these individuals are of special interest to linguists researching how we learn languages.

One such extraordinary language learner who put his remarkable language-learning skills to use in his work was Ken Hale, late Professor of Linguistics at the Massachusetts Institute of Technology. Like Fisher and Dombrowski, he discovered his language learning ability early—as a child he picked up the languages of his classmates and other people around him. Unlike Fisher and Dombrowski, however, he went on to study languages—and the people who speak them—first as a university student and then as a professor. He dedicated his life and research to the pursuit of a greater understanding of how languages are learnt and to the goal of keeping alive some of the world's disappearing languages, many of them languages of oral tradition with no written form.

Much of his research into language learning has taken the form of observing exceptional learners, exploring how they manage to learn not only their native languages, but up to 50 additional languages. In his own study of this area, Professor Hale examined the languages he knew, looking for shared characteristics that might lead to the discovery of laws applicable to all languages.

Professor Hale's real passion, however, was the investigation and preservation of languages in danger of dying out. He travelled far and wide to learn these languages, to find a written form of preserving them, where necessary, and also, at times, to teach them—he taught an Aboriginal language in Australia and a Native American one in the US. He travelled frequently to South America to contribute to the preservation of indigenous languages by learning them and helping encourage indigenous people to see the importance of learning them and of passing them on. He is often quoted in relation to his belief in the importance of this preservation of native languages; he once stated that 'when you lose a language, a large part of the culture goes too, because much of that culture is encoded in the language.'

Hale's work with indigenous people and languages in danger of extinction was also of value in his investigation of the laws governing language learning and his contribution towards a 'universal grammar'. Up to now, however, there has been no proof of such a concept, despite the investigations not only of linguists, but also of neuroscientists and psychiatrists. Work to isolate the part of the brain that deals with language learning has only been partially successful—the left inferior parietal cortex is apparently key to the process, but just how it works is still not understood. And whether the capacity to learn a language is innate and hereditary remains open to question.

Questions 1 – 5

*Match each idea about language learning, 1 – 5, with the correct person, **A – E**, from the box below.*

Who believes that language learning involves:

1   recognising language patterns when listening?   ....

2   learning languages as a baby?   ....

3   an innate ability to learn languages?   ....

4   interacting with others?   ....

5   observing talented language learners?   ....

A	Ken Hale	**D**	Basia Dombrowski
B	Noam Chomsky	**E**	Sandra Fisher
C	Elizabeth Bates		

Questions 6 – 10

Complete the summary below.

Choose the answers from the box and write them in the spaces provided.

extensively	disappear	preserve
universal	~~ability~~	

Ken Hale discovered his **6** .... to learn languages early and made learning languages his profession, dedicating his life to understanding how languages are learnt. The focus of Professor Hale's research was on finding **7** .... principles applying to all languages.

Professor Hale had a passionate interest in the languages which are becoming extinct, and he travelled **8** .... to learn the languages and to help **9** .... them. Hale believed when languages are lost, cultures **10** .... , too.

Questions 11 – 15

Do the following statements agree with the information given in the reading passage?
Next to Questions 11 – 15, write

TRUE	*if the statement is true according to the passage*
FALSE	*if the statement is false according to the passage*
NOT GIVEN	*if the information is not given in the passage*

11   According to Chomsky, all humans have an innate ability
      to learn languages.   ....

12   Cognitive linguists argue that the ability to learn languages
      is genetically determined.   ....

13   Linguists research how people learn languages only by observing children.   ....

14   Professor Hale taught indigenous languages in South America.   ....

15   Scientists study people with speech difficulties to understand how
      the human brain processes language.   ....

ANSWERS AND EXPLANATIONS

Academic Reading Passage 1

1 (need)   Text – …made it clear that governments need to take the issue of global warming very seriously indeed. Paragraph **A**.

2 (an economic)   Text – …examined the issue of climate change from an economic perspective. Paragraph **A**.

3 (disasters/catastrophes)   Text – The report also highlighted a number of catastrophes that would occur… Paragraph **A**.

4 (x)

5 (vii)

6 (ix)

7 (vi)

8 (v)

9 (iv)

10 (iii)

11 (ii)

12 (i)

13 (B)   Text – …the right balance between economic growth and environmental conservation may be achieved. Paragraph **I**.

14 (D)   Text – … the Omgivelse group believes that many of the predictions of the environmentalists are hugely exaggerated. Paragraph **J**.

15 (F)   Text – … than 'quick-fix' measures that would not, he claims, solve the problem. Paragraph **J**.

Academic Reading Passage 2

1 (C)   Text – To the surprise and concern of the scientists conducting the experiment, those individuals taking the supplement—intended to reduce the risk of cancer—were at a significantly higher risk of developing lung cancer. Paragraph 4.

2 (D)   Text – This startling discovery led to the abandonment of the trials mid-way through the experimental process. Paragraph 4.

3 (D)   Text – …the European Medicine Agency (EMEA), have taken the decision to prohibit the production and sale of a number of the higher-dose supplements… Paragraph 6.

4 (B)   Text – …it is essential to keep abreast of new developments in research. Paragraph 8.

5 (False)   Text – Browse the shelves of any health food shop or pharmacy and you'll find dozens of dietary supplements… They are not mentioned as differing. Paragraph 1.

6 (True)   Text – …what antioxidants do is work to neutralise the free radicals in our bodies and later excrete them. Paragraph 2.

7 (Not Given)

8 (Not Given)

9 (Not Given)

10 (True)   Text – …free radicals actually play a role in preventing disease. Paragraph 7.

11 (free radicals)   Text – …the free radicals may help stimulate the antioxidant systems in our bodies. Paragraph 7.

12 (harmful)   Text – …antioxidants and vitamin supplements are of dubious health value at best, and may possibly be harmful. Paragraph 5.

13 (fighting/preventing disease)   Text – …that free radicals may play a fundamental role in the fight against disease. Paragraph 7.

14 (health conscious)   Text – Ironically, those health-conscious individuals who already eat large quantities of fresh fruit and vegetables… Paragraph 8.

15 (approach)   Text – Clearly, then, the use of bottled supplements with your diet is a practice to approach warily… Paragraph 8.

Academic Reading Passage 3

1 (True) Text – Colossus, the first electronic computer … was even more complex and much heavier than its mechanical predecessor. Paragraph 2.

2 (True) Text – It was only when the silicon-based microchip was invented in the early 1950s that computers started to become more compact. Paragraph 3.

3 (Not Given)

4 (False) Text – However, this technology is extremely expensive, so manufacturers are continuing to search for a cheaper alternative. Paragraph 6.

5 (True) Text – …they are able to produce microchips with very few defects. Paragraph 9.

6 (ultraviolet/UV) Paragraphs 5 and 7.

7 (water drop) Paragraph 7.

8 (etching mask) Paragraph 4.

9 (silicon [micro]chip) Paragraph 4.

10 (UV) Paragraph 7.

11 (less than 34) Paragraph 7.

12 (less than 25) Paragraph 6.

13 (nitrogen) Paragraph 4.

14 (water [drops]) Paragraph 7.

15 ([microscopic] mirrors) Paragraph 6.

General Training Reading Passage 1

1 (i)

2 (ix)

3 (vii)

4 (viii)

5 (iv)

6 (ii)

7 (False)	Text – The Güell is not quiet – it's buzzing, … there are no quiet corners! Paragraph **B**.
8 (True)	Text – And room service runs not only to champagne and sushi... Paragraph **C**.
9 (False)	Text – Gracia provides a totally different dining context...Paragraph **D**.
10 (True)	Text – they were flawless – multi-lingual… Paragraph **E**.
11 (Not Given)	
12 (True)	Text – Get online and check out Gracia's website on www.gracia.com; you can book through the website too. Paragraph **G**.
13 ([in] 1870)	Text – ...in a building designed by Antoni Gaudí in 1870...Paragraph **A**
14 ([Güell bar] terrace / from the terrace)	Text – There is a terrace from which to view the sunset... Paragraph **B**.
15 (400€)	Text – ...go for one of the four penthouse suites...At 400€... Paragraph **F**.

General Training Reading Passage 2

1 **(C)**   Text – …offers digital photography courses to all first-year students. Paragraph 1.

2 **(B)**   Text – …course aimed at people with some experience and knowledge of the subject. Paragraph 3.

3 **(B)**   Text – Qualified trainers, graduates from the Media Studies Department… Paragraph 4.

4 **(True)**   Text – …or fill it in online… Paragraph 5.

5 **(Not Given)**

6 **(False)**   Text – Participants are expected to use their own digital cameras, but each participant will have access to a university computer. Paragraph 6.

7 **(False)**   Text – The courses run every month three times a week… Paragraph 6.

8 **(False)**   Text – …earn five credits towards their degree if the course is part of their degree programme. Paragraph 7.

9 **(ii)**

10 **(iii)**

11 **(v)**

12 **(vii)**

13 **(viii)**

14 **(iv)**

15 **(vi)**

16 **(i)**

General Reading Passage 3 Answers

1 (E) Text – 'I just listen for a few minutes, and then I start to speak, and somehow, I just start to see the patterns in my head…' Paragraph 1.

2 (D) Text – 'I'm told that my first words came from four different languages…' Paragraph 2.

3 (B) Text – …language-learning knowledge is 'built in', and that we are hard-wired … to learn a language from birth. Paragraph 4.

4 (C) Text – …that most important is our interaction with other humans and the social environment… Paragraph 5.

5 (A) Text – Much of his research into language learning has taken the form of observing exceptional learners… Paragraph 9.

6 (ability) Text – …he discovered his language-learning ability early. Paragraph 8.

7 (universal) Text – …looking for shared characteristics that might lead to the discovery of laws applicable to all languages… Paragraph 9.

8 (extensively) Text – He travelled far and wide to learn these languages. Paragraph 10.

9 (preserve) Text – He travelled far and wide to learn these languages, to find a written form of preserving them… Paragraph 10.

10 (disappear) Text – …he once stated that 'when you lose a language, a large part of the culture goes too, because much of that culture is encoded in the language'. Paragraph 10.

11 (True) Text – …we are all born with a 'language acquisition device' in our brains… Paragraph 4.

12 (Not Given)

13 (False) Text –… the social environment, and it is this that helps us to learn a language. Paragraph 5.

14 (False) Text – he taught an Aboriginal language in Australia, and a native American one in the US. He traveled frequently to South America to contribute to the preservation of indigenous languages by learning them. Paragraph 10.

15 (Not Given)

CHAPTER 4: THE WRITING MODULE

The Academic Writing and the General Training Writing modules both consist of two tasks that do not require you to have specialised or technical knowledge. The Writing test is designed to assess whether you possess the following skills:

- ability to describe diagrams, tables and lists
- ability to develop an argument supported by evidence
- ability to communicate ideas clearly
- range and accuracy of English vocabulary and sentence structures

You will be given two answer sheets—one for Task 1 and one for Task 2. Answers must be written in full, not in note form. Currently, you can choose whether to write your answers in pen or pencil. You should therefore take a pen, pencil and eraser with you into the exam.

Task 1 carries one-third of the marks. You have to write at least 150 words for Task 1 and are recommended to spend 20 minutes on it.

Task 2 carries two-thirds of the marks. You have to write at least 250 words for Task 2 and are recommended to spend 40 minutes on it. You will lose marks if you write fewer than the required number of words.

The overall result is translated into a score on the IELTS nine-band scale. It is important to follow these guidelines because in both tests. Writing Task 2 carries more marks than Task 1, and you will need to spend the appropriate time on each task to get good marks.

Academic Writing

- Task 1, you must write a report on visual information (graph/table/chart/diagram)
- In Task 2, you are presented with a point of view, an argument or a problem.

General Training Writing

- In Task 1, you must write a letter requesting information or explaining a situation.
- In Task 2, you are presented with a point of view, argument or problem.

ACADEMIC WRITING MODULE TASKS

In the Academic Writing module, the tasks encompass the kind of writing that is common in undergraduate and graduate academic settings.

Writing Task 1

- descriptive report based on visual data, or a process or object

Writing Task 2

- essay based on details of an opinion, an argument or a problem

WRITING TASK 1

You are given a visual input (a chart, graph, table or diagram) and have to transfer the visual information into text using your own words.

For example, you may have to consider a set of statistics presented in a graph or chart, and then summarise it by selecting and reporting the main features. Alternatively, you may have to study a diagram of a device and explain how it works, or you may have to look at a flow chart and describe the main stages in a process.

The target skills in this task are:

- presenting, describing, interpreting, and comparing data
- describing a process or how something works
- using appropriate and accurate language

Writing Task 1 Question Type: Short Descriptive Reports

In Academic Task 1 of the Writing module, you are expected to write a short descriptive report based on visual information or data. This visual information is most commonly presented as line and bar graphs, pie charts or tables.

You might be asked to describe two graphs or charts. If this is the case, you need to compare and contrast the information and make connections between the two.

PIE CHARTS

Pie charts are circular charts divided into sectors or 'pie slices', usually illustrating percentages. The size of each pie slice shows the relative quantity of the data it represents. Together, the slices create a full circle. They are commonly used in the business world and the mass media, and are less common in scientific or technical publications.

EXAMPLE: WRITING TASK 1: PIE CHART

You should spend about 20 minutes on this task.

The chart shows the number of visitors to a local cinema according to age in 2000.

Summarise the information by selecting and reporting the main features, and make comparisons where relevant.

Write at least 150 words.

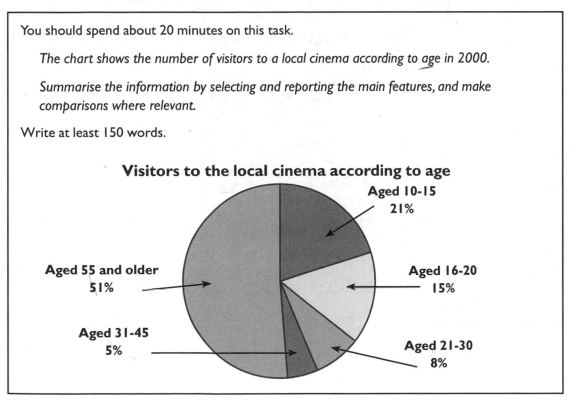

Visitors to the local cinema according to age

Aged 10-15 — 21%
Aged 16-20 — 15%
Aged 21-30 — 8%
Aged 31-45 — 5%
Aged 55 and older — 51%

LINE GRAPHS

Line graphs can be used to show how something changes over time. They have an x-axis (horizontal) and a y-axis (vertical). Usually the x-axis shows the time period and the y-axis shows what is being measured. Line graphs can be used to show trends.

EXAMPLE: WRITING TASK 1: LINE GRAPHS

You should spend about 20 minutes on this task.

The graph below shows the number of people coming to and leaving one European country between 1998 and 2008.

Summarise the information by selecting and reporting the main features, and make comparisons where relevant.

Write at least 150 words.

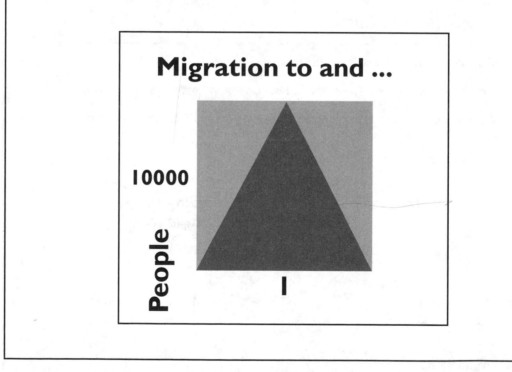

BAR GRAPHS

Bar graphs, also known as bar charts, are similar to line graphs in that they have two axes and are useful for showing how something has changed over a given period of time, especially when there are significant changes. Bar graphs consist of rectangular bars, which can be orientated horizontally or vertically, with the lengths proportional to the data values that they represent. They are typically used for comparing two or more values.

EXAMPLE: WRITING TASK 1: BAR GRAPHS

You should spend about 20 minutes on this task.

The chart below shows the types of film preferred by different age groups at one cinema.

Summarise the information by selecting and reporting the main features, and make comparisons where relevant.

Write at least 150 words.

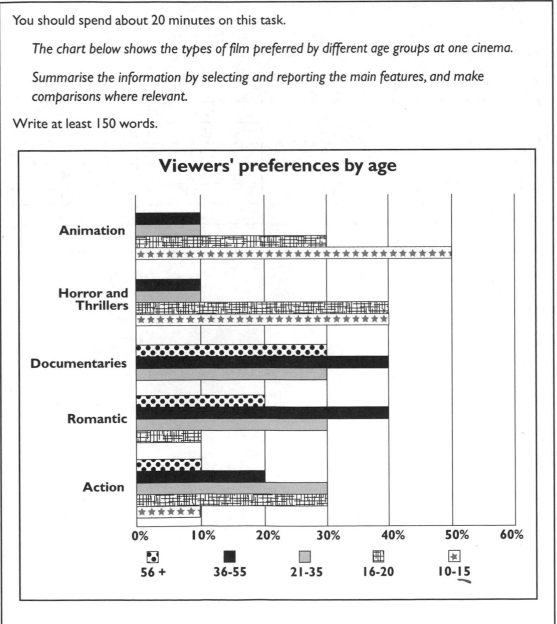

TABLES

Tables contain words and numbers, displayed in columns or boxes to illustrate a set of facts and the relationships among them.

EXAMPLE: WRITING TASK 1: TABLES

You should spend about 20 minutes on this task.

The table below shows the number of language learners who used different modes of learning English between the years 2000 and 2008.

Summarise the information by selecting and reporting the main features, and make comparisons where relevant.

Write at least 150 words.

Modes of learning	Years		
	2000	2004	2008
School	4,000	3,550	2,567
Online	1,567	2,534	5,067
Self-study	2,067	1,523	1,034
Private Classes	2,526	2,344	1,456

Writing Task 1 Question Type: Describing a Process or an Object

Although interpreting and presenting data is the most common task type for Task 1 of the Writing module, two other tasks are possible. In one, you are given a diagram and asked to describe a process or to explain how something works. In the other, you have to describe an object or a series of events.

You might be required to describe an object and how it works or describe and compare two or more objects. This type of task is less common.

EXAMPLE: WRITING TASK 1: DESCRIBE A PROCESS

You should spend about 20 minutes on this task.

The diagram below shows the life cycle of plastic used to produce bottles.

Summarise the information by selecting and reporting the main features, and make comparisons where relevant.

Write at least 150 words.

Life Cycle of Plastic

Cereal

Recycled

Garbage

Glucose   **Fermentation**   **Polymer**   **Plastic bottles**

EXAMPLE: WRITING TASK 1: DESCRIBE AN OBJECT OR EVENT

You should spend about 20 minutes on this task.

The diagram below shows the structure of a basic rocket engine.

Summarise the information by selecting and reporting the main features, and make comparisons where relevant.

Write at least 150 words.

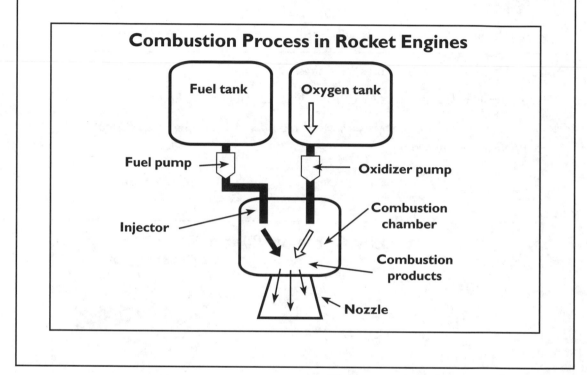

Writing Task 2

You are given brief details of an opinion, an argument or a problem, and have to produce an extended piece of discursive writing in response.

For example, you may have to consider an opinion or weigh the pros and cons of an argument before presenting your own view on the matter. You may also have to discuss various aspects of a problem and then outline your ideas for solving it.

The target skills are:

- arguing, defending or refuting a point of view using supporting evidence
- identifying the causes of or suggesting a solution to a problem
- comparing and contrasting opinions
- evaluating the effects of a course of action

Example: Writing Task 2

You should spend about 40 minutes on this task.

Write about the following topic.

In some countries, young people often decide to work or travel for a time before they start their university studies. Discuss the advantages and disadvantages of doing this.

Give reasons for your answer and include any relevant examples from your own knowledge or experience.

Write at least 250 words.

GENERAL TRAINING WRITING MODULE TASKS

The writing tasks in the General Training module focus on practical business writing issues.

Writing Task 1

- Letter:
  - You must write a letter requesting information or explaining a situation.

Writing Task 2

- Essay:
  - You must produce an piece of discursive writing based on details of an opinion, an argument or a problem

WRITING TASK 1

In this task, a prompt poses a problem or describes a situation that requires a written response in letter format. For example, you may be required to write a letter to an imaginary person such as a friend or a teacher, or it may be a formal letter to a stranger or an official. You are required to use informal, semi-formal or formal writing styles. The style you choose will depend on your relationship to the target reader. Bullet points in the task instructions outline what should be included in the letter.

The task requires you to:

- respond appropriately to a task
- show familiarity with letter-writing styles,
- include the information highlighted in the bullet points
- use appropriate and accurate language

EXAMPLE: WRITING TASK 1

You should spend about 20 minutes on this task.

You are planning to spend a two-week holiday in an English-speaking country where you have a friend. You need some advice about travelling there. Write a letter to your friend. In your letter:

- *explain why you have decided to visit the country and give some details of your trip*

- *ask about the places you should visit*

- *ask if you can stay at your friend's place for a few days*

Write at least 150 words.

WRITING TASK 2

Writing Task 2 is always a discursive essay question that requires you to write about a contemporary social issue. You are given a point of view, an argument or a problem, and are asked for your opinion. The following are some of the typical tasks that you might be required to do:

- Discuss advantages and disadvantages of something.
- Outline the reasons for a problem and suggest solutions.
- Express views on an issue.
- State whether you agree or disagree with a view.
- Take a side in an argument over an issue.

You are required to write an essay which answers all the points in the rubric. The content of the essay must be relevant to the question. The ideas expressed in the essay should be logically organised and supported. Different parts of the essay should be logically and grammatically connected; the essay must be coherent and cohesive.

The target skills are:

- Expressing and justifying a point of view on the topic
- Comparing and contrasting opinions based on personal experience
- Evaluating a situation or development
- Discussing the causes of a problem and suggesting possible solutions

EXAMPLE: WRITING TASK 2

You should spend about 40 minutes on this task.

Write about the following topic:

Some countries invest a lot of money in space research. While some people believe that this money could be better used to solve other problems on Earth, (for example, environmental problems), others argue that space research brings many benefits for life on Earth.

Discuss both of these views and give your own opinion.

Give reasons for your answer and include any relevant examples from your own knowledge and experience.

Write at least 250 words.

SCORING

Academic and General Training scripts are assessed according to the following criteria:

- Task fulfilment: You must follow the instructions and give a clear, accurate and relevant description of the information given in the Task rubric. You must cover all the key points for the task.

- Coherence and cohesion: Your writing needs to be logically organised into paragraphs. Sentences should be logically linked using appropriate conjunctions (and, but, although, that, etc.).

- Vocabulary and grammar: You should use a variety of appropriate vocabulary and sentence structures accurately. Your spelling and punctuation need to be relatively accurate.

ESSENTIAL WRITING SKILLS

In order to write effectively and score well on the Writing module, it is essential to have in-depth knowledge of effective preparation and planning; appropriate style and tone; and the proper structure and format for each type of writing task.

WRITING PROCESS

It is helpful to prepare for the writing tasks using the following procedure:

Stage 1—Preparation

Step 1: Read the task carefully.

Make sure you understand what you are required to write about, and identify the appropriate style and tone for your essay.

Step 2: Brainstorm and note down your ideas.

This should be done on your question paper (but not on the answer sheet) because no one will look at it after the test. Do not write complete sentences. At this point, your notes do not need to follow any logical order. Just write down anything you think is relevant to the task you are given.

Step 3: Plan your essay.

Select, prioritise and group your ideas according to the genre and the suggested layout for your essay.

This stage should not take more than 5 minutes in Task 1 and 10 minutes in Task 2.

Stage 2—Drafting

Step 4: Write your essay following your plan on the answer sheet.

You should use a pencil for this because it will be easier for you to make changes and corrections to your essay later. Make sure that everything you write is legible.

This stage should not take more than 10 minutes in Task 1 and 20 minutes in Task 2, provided the previous stage has been productive.

Stage 3—Reviewing

Step 5: Review and improve your essay.

Check it for grammar and spelling mistakes. You probably will not be able to correct all the mistakes you have made. Focus on locating and correcting your typical mistakes. For this you need to keep a list of such mistakes in mind and use it when you finish writing to check your essay.

This stage should not take more than 5 minutes in Task 1 and 10 minutes in Task 2.

Suggested Checklist for Reviewing

Have you ...

- answered all aspects of the task?
- chosen the appropriate style and tone?
- included an introduction and a conclusion?
- made your paragraphing clear and logical?
- made sure all your supporting points are relevant?
- checked your spelling and grammar?
- written at least 150 words for Task 1 and 250 words for Task 2?

APPROPRIATE STYLE AND TONE

For both parts of the Writing module, the language you use must be consistently appropriate in style and tone.

- **General Training Writing Task 1** should be written in the style appropriate to the task: if it is a letter to a friend, it should be written in a friendly, informal style; if it is a letter to a company or institution, it should be written in a formal style.
- **General Training Writing Task 2** should be written in a semi-formal or formal style.
- **Both Academic Writing Tasks 1 and 2** should be written in a formal and impersonal style.

KAPLAN)

The following are the basic features of formal style:

- All verbs forms must be written in full: do not write contractions such as *can't*, *don't*, etc.

- Do not use abbreviations such as *info* for *information* or *ads* for *advertisements*.

- Avoid using the active voice and the first person singular; in a formal letter you should write: 'A copy of the receipt will forwarded to you as soon as possible' instead of 'I will send you a copy of the receipt asap.'

- Avoid using informal intensifiers such as *really*, *so*, *absolutely*; use *extremely*, *highly*, *entirely*, *fully* instead.

- Avoid using phrasal verbs which tend to be used in informal writing and conversation; for example, use *seek a job* instead of *look for a job*; most phrasal verbs are idiomatic in nature, that is, their meaning cannot usually be inferred from their individual parts.

- Avoid using informal discourse markers and link words such as *besides* or *by the way* and use *incidentally* instead.

- Do not use set phrases and idioms, for example, 'I am not going to pay you a penny' instead of 'Your fee will not be paid.'

- Avoid ellipsis (leaving out words), for example, leaving out the subject *I* in 'Hope to hear from you soon.'

A more academic style will contain all of the features for formal style listed above. In addition, you should do the following:

- Employ more tentative rather than assertive language by:
  - using *possibly* and *probably* in front of verbs and noun phrases: 'This is possibly caused by...' or 'This is probably the most important factor.'
  - using the modal verbs *may* and *might*: 'This may be the most important factor.'
  - using *appears to* and *seems to*: 'This appears to be the most important factor.'
  - avoiding *always* and *every*, and replacing them with *often* and *many/much*.

- Use formal vocabulary, for example, *discuss* rather than *talk about*.

- Use more formal grammar, for example by:
  - using *There* as a subject: 'There is a serious risk of...'
  - using *It* as a subject: 'It is very difficult to...'

- Use an impersonal style by avoiding the use of personal pronouns, for example by:
  - using *One* as a subject: 'One may ask whether...' (*One* is a formal version of *You*)
  - using the passive voice: 'Many things can be done to...' to avoid using *I* and *we*

- Avoid using rhetorical questions: 'Smoking is dangerous. But is banning it such a good idea after all?'

- Avoid the overuse or misuse of certain logical connectors, especially *besides*, *furthermore* and *moreover*. *Besides* is informal, and both *furthermore* and *moreover* mean that the following information is more important than the information before. Use *In addition* or *Also* instead.

Proper Structure for Letters and Essays

The following are outlines and examples of the proper structure for letters and essays that should be used for the IELTS writing tasks.

Letters

Four basic elements that are found in both formal and informal letters: a salutation, an introduction, the body text, and a conclusion with signature.

Let's use a sample Writing Task to illustrate proper letter structure.

> *You have decided to apply for a job as a Spanish instructor that was advertised in the April edition of the magazine* **Teaching Professional**. *This ad was posted by Mr John Sullivan, director of the Spanish department at The Language Institute of Great Britain in London, England. In your letter to Mr Sullivan:*
>
> - **explain why you are writing**
> - **describe your qualifications and experience**
> - **explain how they can contact you**
>
> Write at least 150 words.

Salutation

The salutation is also known as the greeting. Begin your letter with *Dear* followed by the name of the person to whom you are writing. For formal and semi-formal letters, the person's name is followed by a colon. For informal letters, a comma should be used. You do not need to include an address if none was given in the task prompt.

In your letter for the sample task, you are writing to someone you do not know about a possible employment opportunity. Therefore, it is a formal letter; you would have *Dear Mr. Sullivan*: at the top of the answer sheet.

Introduction

In the introduction, you should explain in one or two sentences why you are writing to that person.

In your letter for the sample task, you would explain to Mr. Sullivan that you are interested in the Spanish instructor position.

BODY

The body of the letter is where you will outline the information that you need to communicate, as indicated in the instructions given to you in the prompt. It is important to be concise, but also to include all the necessary information that you have been asked to provide. Your use of advanced and varied vocabulary, as well as a sophisticated and assertive tone, will also illustrate your strong English writing abilities.

In formal and semi-formal letters, you should use a formal conclusion, such as:

- Thank you for your time and assistance. I look forward to hearing from you soon.
- Thank you for your help and consideration. I will call you next week to follow up.

In your letter for the sample task, you would use the body of the letter to describe your qualifications, experience and qualities or competencies relevant to the job, and how you can be contacted, as well as to express gratitude and appreciation to Mr. Sullivan.

CLOSING AND SIGNATURE

The content of the closing will depend on whether the letter is formal or informal. For formal and semi-formal letters in which the name of the addressee is known, the word *Sincerely* followed by a comma should be used. When the name of the addressee is not known, the phrase *Yours faithfully* should be used. For informal letters, other closing words or phrases such as *Regards* or *All the best* can be used. They should also be followed by a comma. Leave some space for your signature, and then write your name in print underneath it

Since the letter for the sample task is a formal letter, you would use the *Sincerely,* closing.

SAMPLE LETTER

Here is a sample letter for the Writing Task:

Dear Mr Sullivan:

I am writing to apply for the post of teacher of Spanish, which I saw advertised in the April edition of the magazine, Teaching Professional. Please find enclosed my CV.

I feel I have many of the important qualifications needed for this job. I have Bachelor's degrees in Spanish and Linguistics, and have worked extensively with young adults, teaching Spanish both in Liverpool, England and Bogotá, Colombia.

My studies at the University of Miami included psychology, linguistics and education, which have given me an in-depth understanding of the behaviour of young adults, as well as the cognitive and psychological factors that affect their learning. The children in my care respect my leadership abilities and I establish excellent working relationships with them and their parents.

In addition, I have considerable experience in organising educational and cultural events, in particular theatrical performances and art displays. I have travelled widely and enjoy meeting new people.

Should you be interested in my qualifications and experience as a teacher, please do not hesitate to contact me at 735-0552.

I look forward to hearing from you.

Sincerely,

Isabella Moreno

Essays

Three basic elements are found in essays: an introduction, the body text, and a conclusion.

Let's use a sample Writing Task to illustrate proper essay structure.

The Internet has dramatically changed the way we access information. Some people think that there is a lot of harmful content with very little regulation online, and argue that strict policies are needed to regulate the Internet. Others oppose this view and think that the Internet should not be regulated.

Discuss both of these views and give your own opinion.

Give reasons for your answer and include any relevant examples from your own knowledge and experience.

Write at least 250 words.

INTRODUCTION

In the introduction, you should include a general or neutral statement about the topic. Avoid using the exact words from the task rubric. Try to paraphrase the statements given in the task. You can include your own opinion if the approach you choose is thesis-led (see explanation on page 151).

BODY

The main body of your essay should have at least two paragraphs which discuss both views. Each paragraph should have a topic sentence and supporting evidence. You should use specific ideas or examples to support the views from the task rubric. Sentences must be logically connected and punctuated. This will help the reader follow your ideas easily.

CONCLUSION

In the last paragraph, you should summarise the main points discussed in the body of your essay and include statements offering a solution, prediction, result or recommendation. You do not need to add new arguments or information, but you can include your point of view in the conclusion.

SAMPLE ESSAY

Here is a sample essay for the Writing Task.

250

Since the Internet became known to the general public in the early 1990s, it has revolutionised the way we access information. Today, even a basic personal computer connected to the Internet and equipped with a browser can be a powerful tool for extracting information from a huge pool of data. There is a genuine concern that information in this data pool is useless, and some can be even harmful. The advocates of this view argue that the Internet should be regulated. Others, however, disagree, and believe that the Internet should not and cannot be regulated.

On the one hand, those in favour of regulating the Internet have valid reasons to be concerned about the safety and the quality of information found on the Web. The Internet does contain websites that incite hatred, racism and religious intolerance. Children surfing the Web may access sites which sell inappropriate or adult content. Also, Internet fraud has increased over the years. Some use these facts to urge governments to adopt strict policies, and in some cases even laws, aimed at banning offensive content from being published online. On the other hand, there are many people who would argue that the Internet is simply a technology platform, and it should be left to the user to decide what information she accesses online. The Internet is a democratic tool which enables everyone to share any kind of information. Therefore, Internet users, especially parents and children, need to be educated about the potential dangers of some information accessible via the Web, and how to protect themselves from coming in contact with offensive online content. Indeed, a quick search will show links to content filters and anti-virus programs which can be downloaded and installed for free, and will make surfing online much safer.

In conclusion, although the dangers online are real, there is no need for the Internet to be regulated by introducing strict policies. I believe the decision to restrict access to harmful online content should be left to individuals.

GENERAL STRATEGIES FOR THE WRITING MODULE

In this section you will find strategies that you can apply to both tasks in the Academic and General Training tests.

Strategy 1: Carefully plan what you will write.

Before you begin writing, you should spend a few minutes analysing and interpreting the factual information. You should look for any interesting features, especially surprising or contrasting information.

For graphs, charts or tables, you should write a brief introduction in your own words using information from the question and the headings or text. For example, include an overview statement about what the data shows. After that, you should focus on key trends, main features and details. Every main feature should be supported by figures from the data. The report should finish with a short summary.

When describing a process, you should study the diagram and make sure you understand how the process works. You need to look for a point where you can begin your description and decide whether the process has an end or whether it is a cycle. You should start with an introductory sentence that summarises the whole process. You should divide your description into paragraphs, especially if there are distinct stages in the process. You can use the notes on the diagram, but should try to paraphrase them in your own words, where possible. You should use sequence expressions such as *first, afterwards, finally*, etc., to link the stages.

Strategy 2: Do not volunteer information you were not asked for.

You are required to report information. Do not speculate or offer an opinion that is outside the given data. Also, you do not need to describe every single change shown in the data, but describe the overall trends. General observations must be supported with specific examples from the data.

Strategy 3: Use varied vocabulary and syntax.

You should use a variety of language to describe trends—for example, verbs with adverbs and nouns with adjectives. The examiner will want to see whether you can deal with the task with flexibility and precision. Showing your ability to use a wide range of vocabulary accurately and appropriately will help you get a higher score for your writing.

For example, say you are analysing the information provided in a chart that shows profits increasing by 50 per cent over two years, a growth that surpassed what the company was expecting. You could use the following adjectives to describe the information:

- Net profits grew exponentially from 2006 to 2008.

- From 2006 to 2008, there was a significant increase in net profits.

- A drastic increase in net profits took place from 2006 to 2008.

Strategy 4: Do not copy the wording in the exam question.

If you do, these words will be deducted from the total number of words and will not be assessed.

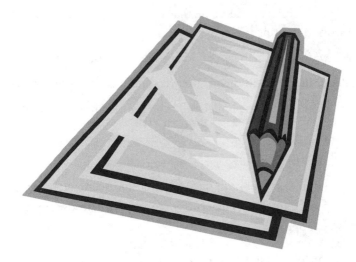

SPECIFIC STRATEGIES FOR WRITING MODULE TASKS

STRATEGIES FOR WRITING TASK 1

Academic Test

- Rather than trying to give reasons for the elements shown in the diagram or describing every detail, concentrate only on significant features.

- Your description should start with a brief overview of the object(s) and its purpose.

- Then focus on how the object works or significant similarities and differences between the objects.

- Vary your language where possible, and use a range of vocabulary and structures.

- Your description should end with a summarising statement.

General Training Test

- Read the question carefully to make sure that you fully understood the function of the letter—the reason for writing it.

- Underline the key words to help you decide on the appropriate style and tone of the letter.

- Study the bullet points given in the instructions and plan what to say about each point.

- Write the letter in full sentences; bullet points and notes are not acceptable in a letter.

STRATEGIES FOR WRITING TASK 2

To answer the question(s) in Task 2 of both the Academic and General Training tests, you need to decide on how to approach the task. There are two options to choose from: an argument-led approach and a thesis-led approach.

For example, compare the following two rubrics:

- Nowadays we are producing more and more garbage. Why do you think this is happening? What can governments do to help reduce the amount of garbage produced? (two questions)

- Nowadays we are producing more and more garbage. What can governments do to help reduce the amount of garbage produced? (one question)

In the first task you are required to give several reasons for 'producing more and more garbage' and to give several solutions, linking these to the reasons you have mentioned before. Therefore, you will probably use the argument-led approach.

In the second task you are asked only one question. The thesis-led approach would be the most suitable for this task.

Argument-Led Approach

The argument-led approach is useful when discussing different views, comparing advantages and disadvantages, or analysing problems and suggesting solutions. You must show that you can summarise and evaluate the argument logically, supporting both opinions with clear supporting evidence.

Step 1: Underline key words in the exam question.

This will help you focus your answer on the key points, then brainstorm ideas for both sides of the argument, that is, both for and against the issue.

Here is a sample task rubric with the words underlined:

> _Celebrities_ such as actors, athletes and musicians earn _large salaries_ compared to _other professionals_. Some people consider this _unfair_, while others think that celebrities _deserve_ to be paid a lot for the work they do.
>
> Discuss _both_ points of view and give _your opinion_ on the subject.

Step 2: Show clear links between the main argument and the supporting arguments.

In your introduction, re-word the question showing the topic clearly and state the opinion(s) that you will go on to discuss.

Here's a sample introduction statement:

> Famous movies stars, popular musicians and athletes often get paid a lot more than other professionals. While this may not seem fair to many, it is a matter of debate with several strong arguments for and against celebrities earning a lot more than people in other professions.

Remember that each paragraph should have one main argument—start a new paragraph when you start a new main idea. Develop contrasting views, problems and solutions, advantages and disadvantages. Make sure you justify each point with clear supporting material. Do not forget to provide a logical argument wherever you refute the opposing opinion.

Here is a sample of two body paragraphs.

On the one hand, celebrities who work in multi-billion-dollar industries such as cinema or sport help to generate a lot of jobs. For example, such events as rock concerts create employment opportunities for people working in catering, logistics and publishing. Some of the money famous people receive is put to a good cause. It is not uncommon for celebrities to give generous donations to charity organisations and to participate in charity fund-raising events.

On the other hand, those who think that paying huge amounts to celebrities is unfair may argue that famous people do not have much to offer except their image. Their success and popularity do not result from many years of academic study or experience, but are created by the media and celebrity-crazed culture.

Step 3: Provide a strong conclusion.

Conclude your essay by summarising the main points and stating your own personal view.

Here is a sample conclusion:

In conclusion, it is debatable whether many celebrities' large salaries are justified, and both critics and advocates seem to have plenty of arguments in support of their views. I personally think that famous people's salaries should be proportional to the amount of money their talent helps to generate.

Thesis-Led Approach

The thesis-led approach is more effective when you are asked only one question or when you have a very clear opinion on the subject.

Step 1: Underline key words in the exam question.

This will help you focus your answer on the key points, then brainstorm ideas for both sides of the argument, that is, both for and against the issue.

Step 2: Show clear links between the main argument and the supporting arguments.

State your opinion clearly in the introduction and use the subsequent paragraphs to justify and support your point of view. Your introduction should consist of the following elements:

- the opinion or problem you are asked to discuss
- your thesis

Here is a sample introduction statement:

> Athletes, actors, and musicians all over the world earn large sums of money, while professionals in other very important areas receive only a fraction of such incomes. Some people believe this is not fair, while others argue that it is quite logical and acceptable. It is my belief that most professionals in sports and the entertainment industry receive salaries that reflect the value of their work, and it is therefore justifiable.

Body paragraphs should contain a main or topic statement with supporting points. The topic statement is usually, but not always, in the first sentence of the paragraph.

Here is a sample body paragraph. The number 1 indicates a main idea and/or topic, while the number 2 indicates supporting points:

> Some people think these celebrities should earn more because they pay more in taxes[1], and their work helps generate more jobs[1] for other people. That is why entertainment is often called an industry. It involves thousands of people working on[2] organising concerts, producing audio and video recordings, and doing other related work.

Step 3: Provide a strong conclusion.

The objective of the conclusion is usually to (re)state your final opinion. Your conclusion must logically follow the arguments you have presented in the body paragraphs. It should not contain any points or explanations, or add any new information. It should never lead to another discussion.

Here is a sample conclusion:

> On balance, having considered the points employed by both sides of the argument, I feel that the income that these stars receive is proportional to the economic benefits they create.

WRITING MODULE PRACTICE SECTIONS

In this section, you will find full-length practice sections for the Academic and General Training Writing modules. Write your answers on a separate piece of paper. You can make notes on the pages in the book.

GO ON TO THE NEXT PAGE

ACADEMIC WRITING MODULE PRACTICE SECTION 1

Task 1

You should spend about 20 minutes on this task.

The chart below shows the estimated literacy rates by region and gender for 1999–2004.

Summarise the information by selecting and reporting the main features, and make comparisons where relevant.

Write at least 150 words.

	Total	Male	Female
World	82.2	87.2	77.3
Africa	62.5	71.6	53.9
Americas	93.6	94.1	93.2
Asia	79.3	85.9	72.5
Europe	98.8	99.2	98.5
Oceania	93.4	94.2	92.7

Task 2

You should spend about 40 minutes on this task.

Write about the following topic:

For a long time there has been concern about the quality of the food we eat because of additives and contaminants. Recently, genetically modified food is becoming more common and is causing concern. Is this concern justified or not?

Give reasons for your answer and include any relevant examples from your own knowledge and experience.

Write at least 250 words.

ACADEMIC WRITING MODULE PRACTICE SECTION 2

Task 1

You should spend about 20 minutes on this task.

The chart below shows the results of a survey into the causes of poor school attendance in the UK in 2007.

Summarise the information by selecting and reporting the main features, and make comparisons where relevant.

Write at least 150 words.

Causes of Poor Attendance in UK Schools in 2007

Legend:
- Upbringing
- Both parents working
- Lack of school discipline
- Peer group pressure
- Bullying

Percentages shown: 5%, 40%, 25%, 15%, 15%

Task 2

You should spend about 40 minutes on this task.

Write about the following topic:

Some people think that the government should provide unemployed people with a free mobile phone and free access to the Internet to help them find jobs.

To what extent you agree or disagree with this opinion? Give reasons for your answer and include any relevant examples from your own knowledge and experience.

Write at least 250 words.

KAPLAN

GENERAL TRAINING WRITING MODULE PRACTICE SECTION 1

Task 1

You should spend about 20 minutes on this task.

You have a friend who lives in a city abroad. You have decided that you would like to apply to do a course at one of the colleges in this city. Write a letter to your friend. In your letter:

- *explain what you would like to do*

- *explain what kind of work or studies you have been doing for the past few years*

- *ask for assistance in contacting an appropriate institution*

Write at least 150 words.

Task 2

You should spend about 40 minutes on this task.

Write about the following topic:

Some people think that recent innovations in technology have made life more comfortable and helped us to be more efficient by saving us time, while others argue that technology has made us less efficient.

Discuss both these views and give your own opinion.

Give reasons for your answer and include any relevant examples from your own knowledge and experience.

Write at least 250 words.

GENERAL TRAINING WRITING MODULE PRACTICE SECTION 2

Task 1

You should spend about 20 minutes on this task.

The Local Council in the area where you live has decided to demolish an old historical building to build a shopping centre. Write a letter to the head of the Council. In your letter:

- *explain why it is important to preserve the old building*

- *suggest how the building can be used to benefit the local community*

- *suggest another place for the shopping centre*

Write at least 150 words.

Task 2

You should spend about 40 minutes on this task.

Write about the following topic:

In some countries, people spend a lot of money on their pets. They buy special food for their cats or dogs, buy them toys and often pay high fees for medical treatment.

Some people think this is a waste of money.

What are the advantages and disadvantages of having a pet? Do people spend too much money on pets?

Give reasons for your answer and include any relevant examples from your own knowledge and experience.

Write at least 250 words.

MODEL ANSWERS

Before you look at the model answers below, look at your answers and use the check lists for Task 1 and Task 2 below to analyse your responses to the tasks in the Practice Section.

Task 1 Check List

- Have you followed the instructions exactly?
- Have you covered all aspects of the task and included all the key elements required?
- Are the tone and the style (formal, informal) appropriate and consistent?
- Is your writing well-organised into paragraphs?
- Does each paragraph have a clear central idea?
- Is there a clear introduction or overview?
- Have you used a variety of vocabulary?
- Are your sentences well structured?
- Are your sentences well linked? Have you used grammatical and logical connectors?
- Is your handwriting legible?

Task 2 Check List

- Have you discussed the ideas from the task rubric?
- Are the arguments developed and supported with relevant examples?
- Have you expressed your point of view?
- Have you logically organised your ideas into paragraphs using connectors?
- Does your essay have a clear introduction and conclusion?
- Have you used a variety of vocabulary and sentence structures?
- Have you punctuated the sentences accurately?
- Are some of the sentences too long or too short?
- Is your writing reasonably accurate?
- Have you used word order, verb tenses, prepositions and articles accurately?
- Is your handwriting legible?

ACADEMIC WRITING MODULE PRACTICE SECTION 1

Task 1

The graph describes estimated literacy rates for men and women in 2000-2004 [1999] in five regions: Africa, the Americas, Asia, Europe and Oceania. It also shows average world literacy rates for both genders for the same years.

According to the graph, Europe has the highest literacy rates, reaching almost 99 per cent. There is virtually no difference in literacy rates for European men and women.

In Oceania and the Americas, the figures for both men and women are almost the same. In both regions over 93 per cent of the population is literate.

In both Asia and Africa, there are considerable differences in literacy rates between men and women. In Asia, only 72.5 per cent of women are literate, whereas the figure for Asian men is 13 per cent higher. In Africa, the gap is nearly double, with 53.9 of all African women being literate and 71.6 of the African men being able to read and write.

Overall, around 82 per cent of the world population is literate. In Europe, Oceania and the Americas the literacy rates are the highest, with over 90 per cent of the population able to read and write. Asia and Africa have lower literacy rates than the other regions in the graph.

(207 words)

about tense

Task 2

Many people today are concerned about the quality of the food they eat. This concern has lead to an increasing number of organic products appearing on supermarket shelves. Many people refuse to buy products that contain artificial colourings or preservatives, or foods that come from genetically modified crops, fearing that these foods are unhealthy and can cause cancer and other diseases. Some advocates of genetically modified (GM) food consider such attitudes unjustified. I am one of them, and in this essay I will try to justify why I think concerns about GM foods have little merit.

First of all, GM foods have been around for almost 20 years. Contrary to the claims of those opposed to GM foods, there have not been any registered cases of such foods causing cancer or any other diseases. In fact, research into GM foods has been unable to confirm any harmful effects on human health whatsoever.

Secondly, not everyone can afford organic foods. Climate change and rising fuel costs have lead to global increases in the price of food, and as a result, many poor people are spending more money on feeding themselves. Many can barely afford to buy food. GM plants are generally more resistant to droughts, floods and pests, and have higher yields per hectare, which leads to more affordable food prices.

The world population keeps growing and is expected to reach eight billion by 2015. People in fast-developing countries such as India and China are consuming more energy and food. The only practical solution to the ever-increasing demand for food is to grow more GM crops. Unless scientists and governments come up with a better solution, GM foods are here to stay.

To conclude, people are free to eat the food of their choice, be it organic or not. However, I think that many people overlook the major benefits of GM foods, and instead choose to focus on the unproven negative effects of such foods.

(324 words)

ACADEMIC WRITING MODULE PRACTICE SECTION 2

Task 1

According to a recent survey in the UK, people attribute poor attendance in schools to a number of causes. The respondents were asked to choose from five causes: upbringing, both parents working, lack of school discipline, peer group pressure, and bullying.

First, the way a child is brought up was considered by about 40 per cent of respondents to be a cause of poor attendance. Among the five causes suggested in the survey, this was the opinion most commonly held, whereas only 25 per cent of those asked thought having both parents working might lead to children missing school.

Second, about 15 per cent of people surveyed thought lack of school discipline might also be a contributing factor. The same number of people thought that peer group pressure was a cause of poor attendance.

Bullying was not widely seen to be an important cause, with only five per cent of respondents considering it a cause of poor school attendance.

According to the data shown, it appears that poor attendance in schools in the UK is not seen as being attributable to only one category of causes.

(186 words)

Task 2

Digital technology has changed the way people access information. Since their introduction in the 80s, technologies such as mobile phones and the Internet have become cheap and commonplace. Some people see this as a window of opportunity to deal effectively with such problems as unemployment. They argue that the government should make mobile phones and the Internet available free of charge to anyone looking for a job. I disagree with this point of view for several reasons.

In the first place, one of the most common reasons why jobless people cannot find employment is that the skills they have are not needed or out of date. Instead of investing public funds in an expensive infrastructure or distributing mobile phones for free to those out of work, the government should organise training programmes that people who are out of work could sign up for in order to learn new skills.

Another argument against the idea is the way the use of the Internet and mobiles phones would be controlled. It would be technically very challenging to control how these technologies are used. Instead, public money could be used to provide subsidised bus or subway tickets for the unemployed who, for example, need to travel for a job interview.

Moreover, it would be prohibitively expensive to maintain such a system and ensure that it worked properly. The government could invest public funds into training courses for the staff working in job centres to make them more efficient at helping the unemployed to find jobs.

To sum up, I am convinced that public money should not be wasted on expensive technology, and can be better used to deal with the problem of unemployment by giving the unemployed free and better-quality training.

(288 words)

GENERAL TRAINING WRITING MODULE PRACTICE SECTION 1

Task 1

Dear John,

Sorry I haven't written to you for so long. I have been very busy over the last year and I never seem to get a minute to myself.

I'd like to study electrical engineering in Australia and I hope you can give me some advice. I think I would prefer Melbourne because I know you and a few people from my visit there last year.

This year I'm doing maths and physics at school and I hope to do well in my exams. However, I really don't know which university to apply to, so could you send me some information about different colleges? Also, can you find out what qualifications I need, please? For instance, as an overseas student, do I have to take an English test?

I hope you don't mind doing this for me. It's much better to get this information from someone who lives in the country, so I hope to hear from you soon.

Many thanks,

Andrew

(163 words)

Task 2

Technology has existed as long as mankind has, but the pace of technological innovation has never been as fast as it is nowadays. New gadgets which promise to make life easier and more comfortable are launched on a daily basis. We are coaxed into buying electronic devices by high-tech companies which promise that their technologies can help us become more efficient.

On the one hand, it is true that technology makes life more comfortable. It is hard to imagine life without such appliances as the vacuum cleaner or the washing machine. The invention of the microchip has enabled engineers to shrink electronic devices to the sizes which make them practical to use. Huge computers which used to take up an entire room in 1950s have evolved into tiny pocket-size devices which are infinitely more complex than their early prototypes. Communication technologies such as the Internet enable us to be connected 24 hours a day, seven days a week.

On the other hand, technology is a major cause of stress for those who rely heavily on it. The more complex technological inventions become, the more prone they are to malfunctioning. For example, a broken hard drive can cause a disruption to a project or can bring it to a complete halt for days or even weeks.

As technologies become more sophisticated, people need to spend more time learning how to use them. Quite often by the time technology users have figured out how to use an invention, a new technology comes along to replace the old one, and the cycle begins again.

In conclusion, technological inventions do make life more comfortable. However, I do not believe they make us more effective or efficient unless we learn how to use them properly, which is rarely the case.

(295 words)

GENERAL TRAINING WRITING MODULE PRACTICE SECTION 2

Task I

Dear Sir or Madam:

I am writing to express my dissatisfaction with the Local Council's decision to demolish the old City Hall building in the Lake Gardens area where I have lived for five years.

Although the building is in a very poor condition, I do not think it is beyond repair. I believe that the old City Hall can be restored and put to good use for the local community.

It can be used to house a library or a community centre for the people living in the area. I am convinced that you would have no shortage of people who would gladly volunteer to organise a fund-raising campaign for the cause.

I understand that the proposed shopping centre is going to bring business and jobs to the area, but I do not think this should be done at the expense of losing one of the oldest and most interesting historical landmarks in Lake Gardens. I wonder if the Council has considered the abandoned brick factory on the corner of the Maple Street and Hillside Lane as a possible site for the construction project.

I hope the Lake Gardens Local Council reconsiders the decision to demolish the old City Hall and finds a different site for building the shopping centre.

Yours faithfully,

John Smith

(215 words)

Task 2

Many people keep a dog or cat or some other kind of pet in their homes. Although there is some expense involved in terms of good food and medical treatment, there are still many benefits to keeping a pet.

First of all, pets are good companions. This is especially important for people who live alone and for older people who do not go out much. Some pets can also help to protect the house from burglars. Second, dogs and cats like to play and can give hours of fun to children and adults. Children can also learn to be responsible when taking care of an animal, and it also helps them to be more mature and reliable. Finally, the actual expense of feeding pets is not that high as they can eat the leftovers from family meals.

Some people claim that keeping pets is not hygienic. I do not think this is necessarily true. Responsible pet owners keep their pets clean and healthy so they do not smell bad. People also say that certain pets, such as large dogs, can be dangerous. Indeed there have been cases of dogs attacking and seriously injuring children. However, these attacks are rare, and are often the result of irresponsible owners who either do not train their dogs properly or actually train them to be aggressive. So, the issue of pets being unclean or dangerous is in fact often created by the owners, not the pets themselves.

To sum up, there are more benefits than drawbacks to keeping a pet, especially for elderly people and children. In most cases, therefore, the cost is justified.

(270 words)

CHAPTER 5:   THE SPEAKING MODULE

The IELTS Speaking module assesses the communicative and linguistic skills necessary for effective oral communication between non-native and other speakers of English in educational, training and social contexts. Candidates are assessed individually by one trained examiner.

The activities in each part are designed to collect samples of your speaking performance. Your speaking skill is assessed with a set of Speaking Test Descriptors spanning nine bands, from the Non-User of the language at Band 1 to the Expert User at Band 9. Both Academic and General Training candidates follow the same format for all parts of the speaking test.

You are assessed according to the following criteria:

Fluency and Coherence
- ability to express ideas clearly and coherently without long hesitations

Lexical Resources
- range of vocabulary used
- appropriate use of vocabulary

Grammatical Range and Accuracy
- range of structures used
- number of errors

Pronunciation
- whether it is easy to understand what you are saying
- ability to use features of English pronunciation (intonation, stress and connected speech) naturally
- accents are not taken into consideration

PARTS OF THE SPEAKING MODULE

The test takes between 11 and 14 minutes and consists of three parts. The examiner is responsible for the timing in all parts of the test.

In Parts 1 and 2, the examiner follows a script with instructions and questions. During Part 3 of the speaking test, the examiner will paraphrase question prompts to match them to your proficiency level. Each test is recorded for security and monitoring purposes.

Part 1: Introduction and Interview

- Lasts 4–5 minutes

- Examiner asks questions based on topic frames.

- Topics are general, such as your home, family, job or interests.

Part 2: Individual Long Turn

- Lasts 3–4 minutes

- You are given a topic card and 1 minute to prepare notes.

- You speak a monologue based on the topic card.

Part 3: Two-way Discussion

- Lasts 4–5 minutes

- Examiner asks you questions based on the topic from Part 2.

- You may be asked up to seven questions, which the examiner adapts to your proficiency level.

PART 1—INTRODUCTION

The examiner introduces himself or herself, and then asks questions about familiar topics, such as your home, family, job and interests. This part lasts 4–5 minutes.

The examiner will ask you questions about yourself based on different topics, usually three questions on each topic. Each set of questions on a specific topic is called a 'Topic Frame'.

The first topic is often about where you live, your work or your studies. The two other topics will be randomly selected from a list of eight topics available to the examiner. Although topics may be similar from one test version to another, the questions included in the Topic Frames will be different.

EXAMPLE OF TOPIC FRAME 1

Examiner:	Let's talk about your home (in your country).
	• What type of house or flat do you live in?
	• What do you like about living there?
	• What types of accommodation are typical in your country?
	• What type of accommodation would you like to live in the future?

EXAMPLE OF TOPIC FRAME 2 OR 3:

Examiner:	Now let's talk about animals.
	• Are there many different kinds of animals in your country?
	• How do people in your country generally treat animals?
	• Do you think people should do more to protect animals? [Why/Why not?]
	• Do animals mean anything special in your culture?

When the examiner has finished asking questions about the first topic, he or she will move on to another general topic by saying: 'Now let's talk about …' or 'Let's talk about …'. Some topics might be relatively sensitive and personal in their nature, so the examiner might say something like this:

Examiner:	Now let's talk about family. Are you happy to do that?

PART 2—INDIVIDUAL LONG TURN

You will be required to speak for one to two minutes. The examiner gives you a card that contains a topic and some bullet point prompts. Before speaking, you will have one minute to prepare and make notes on a sheet of paper. When you are finished speaking, the examiner will ask one or two questions to wrap up the long turn. This part lasts 3–4 minutes.

You will not be allowed to bring any pens, pencils or paper into the examination room—these will be provided by the examiner. The notes are not marked and will be destroyed after the test. You cannot take them out of the room. While you are making notes, the examiner will not talk to you.

Part 2 will begin when the examiner says something like this: 'Now, I'm going to give you a topic and I'd like you to talk about it for one to two minutes. Before you talk, you'll have one minute to think about what you are going to say. You can make some notes if you wish. Do you understand?'

EXAMPLE: TASK CARD

Describe a piece of furniture you have in your home.

You should say:

- **What kind it is and what you use it for**
- **What materials it is made of**
- **How this piece of furniture was chosen for your home**

Also explain how you feel about this piece of furniture.

PART 3—TWO-WAY DISCUSSION

In Part 3 of the Speaking Test, the examiner will ask you to discuss some abstract, non-personal questions that he or she raises. Depending on your level of English and performance, you might be asked up to seven questions on a variety of themes related to the topic of furniture, for example, buying furniture, furniture style and design, and so on. You are not required or expected to ask the examiner any questions. This part lasts 4–5 minutes.

EXAMPLE: TWO-WAY DISCUSSION QUESTIONS

Examiner:	We've been talking about a piece of furniture you have in your home and I'd like to discuss with you one or two more general questions related to this. Let's consider first of all buying furniture. Who usually makes decisions about what furniture to buy in your culture?

Examiner:	Could you compare the criteria that people use when choosing furniture for their homes and for their offices?
	Can you describe some recent changes in the design of furniture in your country?
	In what ways does the design of a place or furniture affect how people feel?

EXAMPLE: MORE TWO-WAY CONVERSATION QUESTIONS WITH RESPONSES

Examiner:	Do you think living in a big city is better than living in a small town?
Candidate:	I don't think living in a large city has more advantages than living in a small town. Living in a small town is, in my opinion, much less dangerous than living in a big city. Also, I am convinced that it is much healthier and less stressful. Some of my family members, for example, live in a small town. For some reason, they seem to me much happier and more energetic than my brothers and I, who live in the capital.

Examiner:	Why do some people think it is good idea to make it compulsory to study a foreign language at school?
Candidate:	It's probably because many parents realise that their children are not mature enough to understand the value and advantages of being able to communicate in a foreign language. Other people might consider it a good way to exercise their children's minds.

GENERAL STRATEGIES FOR THE SPEAKING MODULE

Strategy 1: Don't memorise long answers.

Anything you say that the examiner thinks has been memorised will not be assessed.

Strategy 2: Use your imagination in your answers.

Remember that the examiner is testing your ability to speak English, not your views or general knowledge.

Strategy 3: Use varied and advanced vocabulary.

You must show that you have enough vocabulary to discuss non-personal topics. The examiner will be checking to see if you can use complex sentences. You will get credit for your attempts, even if you make mistakes.

Strategy 4: You can stall, but not for long.

If you cannot think of an answer to an examiner's question right away, you can say some 'filler' phrases to acknowledge the question and to show the examiner that are thinking about your answer. However, avoid waiting too long before you speak. This will cause the examiner to give you lower marks for fluency.

Here are some phrases you can use to fill in the spaces when you need more time:

- That's a good question!
- OK, well, let me see.
- I've never thought of this before …
- Hmm, let me think …

Strategy 5: Make your voice heard.

You should speak loudly enough for the examiner to hear you and for the tape-recorder to capture what you are saying. Also, make sure to pronounce your words as clearly and correctly as possible.

SPECIFIC STRATEGIES FOR THE SPEAKING MODULE

PART 1

In this part of the test, the examiner will ask you some questions about yourself. You should not feel nervous or threatened in any way. The examiner is there to help you speak, and if you misunderstand a question or cannot answer, he or she will repeat or change the question.

Strategy 1: Ask to clarify questions you do not understand.

It is OK to ask questions if you do not understand what the examiner has asked you. This will not lower your score.

Strategy 2: Give direct answers to the examiner's questions.

Answer each question you are asked. Try to give examples, reasons and your opinions where appropriate. Your answers do not need to be very long or sophisticated.

Strategy 3: Try to sound natural.

Try not to be nervous. Speak to the examiner as if you were speaking to someone you have just been introduced to.

PART 2

You will have one minute to prepare and make notes. It is important to make useful notes to guide you during your turn. Do not try to write out your whole speech. Write down your ideas and some key points. The three bullet points on your task card will help you do this.

Strategy 1: Read the Task Card carefully.

You don't want to misread or misunderstand the topic or bullet points. If you rush this step, you might makes notes and prepare a speech that doesn't cover the topic at all. Then you'll have to talk without any preparation.

Strategy 2: Make brief notes about each point on the card.

During the minute you are given to prepare for this turn, decide how you will introduce and link your ideas. Keep your answer relevant to the instructions on the card and try to address each point in turn. Remember to include some examples to support what you say.

Do not try to write these as full sentences because there will not be enough time for this. Write key words only, starting each point on a new line for clarity. You should include key words and expressions and prompt words to help you remember your ideas.

Strategy 3: Keep to the time limit.

You are expected to speak for a maximum of two minutes, but you will not be timed. One to two minutes can seem like a long time, so you do need to have an idea before taking the test of how much you can say in two minutes. That way you can make sure to cover all the points on the Task Card without going under or over.

The best way to prepare for this is to practise writing down notes and crafting speeches that last roughly one to two minutes. Use the points on the card to help you organise what you are going to say.

EXAMPLE: TASK CARD, NOTES, SPEECH, AND WRAP-UP QUESTIONS

Describe a piece of furniture you have in your home.

You should say:

- **What kind it is and what you use it for**
- **What materials it is made of**
- **How this piece of furniture was chosen for your home**

Also explain how you feel about this piece of furniture.

Notes

- writing desk—bedroom
- antique, expensive
- oak
- got it from grandparents—don't know much about it
- took good care, doesn't look shabby
- used it for school
- love it—will give to my children or collector of antiques

Speech

I would like to talk about my writing desk. This desk is in my bedroom. It is an antique and is probably very expensive. It is quite large and I think it is made of oak. I received it as a present from my grandparents when they moved into my parents' house. I do not know much about how long my grandparents had it or where it came from. It's quite old, but I have taken really good care of it, so it doesn't really look shabby. It's got three drawers. Some parts of it are decorated with some fancy carvings. Anyway, I really love this desk because I spent lots of time studying and working at it when I was at school. I still find it very useful and will probably give it to my children when they start school. If they don't want it, I'll sell it to a collector of antiques.

Wrap-up Questions

After you have completed this task, you will be asked a couple of rounding-off questions, which require very simple answers.

Examiner:	Do any of your friends have a piece of furniture like this?
Candidate:	Yes, some of them do.

Examiner:	Where would you go to buy a piece of furniture like this?
Candidate:	At an antique shop.

PART 3

In this part, the examiner wants to hear you discuss some general but more abstract topics that are related to Part 2.

During this part of the Speaking module, you will be expected to show your ability to:

- fully answer the examiner's specific questions on a specific topic
- introduce and connect your ideas
- express and justify your opinions on a range of topics

The examiner can only assess what you say, not what you are thinking, so it is important to give a full and relevant answer, linking your ideas smoothly. This skill is known as *fluency*.

Strategy 1: Speak at length, but stay on topic.

In the Speaking test, you should try to give a 'full' or extended answer. The examiner cannot give you high marks if your responses are always very short. However, make sure that the information you provide is relevant to the question and that you have kept to the original topic of the question.

EXAMPLE: RESPONSES TO A PART 3 QUESTION

Examiner:	Do you take photographs?
Candidate 1:	Yes, I do.
Candidate 2:	Yes, I like photography. I especially enjoy taking photographs using my digital camera. There's so much I can do with those photos on my computer.
Candidate 3:	Yes, I like photography. I also like drawing and painting. I started painting when I was 12 years old.

Candidate 1 has given a short, limited answer that will not receive high marks. Candidate 3 has added information that is not relevant to the topic. The best answer is from Candidate 2, who has given an extended answer that is relevant to the question and conversation topic.

If you give a short reply, the examiner will ask more questions to help you develop your answer. He or she may stress some words to help you. However, you will get much better marks if the examiner does not need to help you with providing appropriate answers.

Strategy 2: Learn key phrases for introducing and linking ideas.

To make your speech easier to understand and follow, use a variety of expressions and words that help introduce and link your ideas. Here are some helpful phrases.

- **Presenting your point of view:**
  - I think that …
  - I don't think that …
  - Personally, …
  - I believe …

- As far as I understand/know, …
- I am convinced that …
- In my opinion, …
- I personally think …
- I guess …
- I suppose …
- I'd say …

- **Adding new ideas or statements**

  - Also, …
  - And …

- **Explaining reasons and consequences**

  - It's probably because …
  - That's why …
  - One of the reasons for this could be …
  - What this means is that …

- **Speculating**

  - might
  - may
  - could
  - perhaps
  - It's not likely that …
  - It's very unlikely that …

- **Moving to the next point**

  - Anyway, …
  - So, to move on, …

- **Giving examples**

  - For example, …
  - For instance, …

Strategy 3: Express and justify your opinions correctly and with confidence.

In this part of the Speaking module, you will need to communicate your opinions while also demonstrating your control of grammatical structures and depth of vocabulary. Use modal verbs to give possible reasons or describe likely advantages/disadvantages.

Examiner:	Why do you think some people like giving presents more than receiving?
Candidate:	Well, it *might* be because they are generous. Another reason *could be* they feel good about themselves when they give someone a present.

When you give an opinion, support it by giving a reason for it or by offering a second point of view.

Examiner:	Do you agree that public transport should be free?
Candidate:	I totally agree. We all pay taxes and I think some of the money governments collect from tax-payers should be invested in building an efficient public transport system. This could also encourage people to use public transport instead of driving private cars. But I think it might be difficult and very expensive to put this idea into practice, and I suppose many people would disagree that making public transport free is a good idea.

SPEAKING MODULE PRACTICE SECTIONS

In this section, you will find three full-length practice sections for the Speaking Module. The best way to use the practice sections is to practise speaking with a friend who speaks good English and who can use the questions to interview you.

It is a good idea to record the practice interviews and listen to them. This can help you build up your confidence. You can also read out the questions and record them using a cassette or digital recorder. Then you can play back the recording, pause it after each question and practise answering the questions this way.

GO ON TO THE NEXT PAGE

PRACTICE SECTION 1

Part 1 (4–5 minutes)

In this part, the examiner will ask you 2–3 general questions about yourself:

- Where do you live?

- Do you work or study?

- Where do you work? / Where do you study?

- What do you like doing in your free time? Do you have any hobbies?

- Do you cook? How often do you cook?

Part 2 (3–4 minutes)

The examiner will give you a topic card, a pencil and some paper. You will be given one minute to prepare what you are going to say. You can make notes if you wish to plan your answer. Then the examiner will ask you to speak about the topic for one to two minutes.

Describe a city or a town you have enjoyed visiting.

You should say:

- **when you visited the town or the city**
- **what you did there**
- **how long you stayed there**

and explain why you enjoyed the visit.

After your talk, the examiner will ask you one or two brief questions about the topic.

- Would you like to visit the place again?

- Has anyone you know visited the city/town?

Part 3 (4–5 minutes)

In this part, the examiner will ask you 2–3 general questions related to the topic in Part 2:

Travel and Tourism

- Do people travel more nowadays than they used to in the past?
- What can one learn from travelling to other countries?
- Do you think people will travel more, or less, in the future?
- Tourism, economy and environment

Tourism, Economy and Environment

- What positive or negative effects does tourism have on a local economy?
- What effects does travel have on the environment?
- What can countries do to promote tourism?

Practice Section 2

Part 1 (4–5 minutes)

In this part, the examiner will ask you 2–3 general questions about yourself:

- Do you live in a house or a flat?
- How long have you lived there?
- Do you like shopping? What kinds of things do you like buying?
- Do you like listening to music? When do you listen to music?

Part 2 (3–4 minutes)

The examiner will give you a topic card, a pencil and some paper. You will be given one minute to prepare what you are going to say. You can make notes if you wish to plan your answer. Then the examiner will ask you to speak about the topic for one to two minutes.

Describe a film you saw and really liked.

You should say:

- **the name of the film**
- **when and where you saw it**
- **what the film was about**

and explain why you liked the film.

After your talk, the examiner will ask you one or two brief questions about the topic.

- Have you recommended this film to anyone? Why / Why not?
- Would you like to see the film again?

Part 3 (4–5 minutes)

In this part, the examiner will ask you 2–3 general questions related to the topic in Part 2:

Cinema and Entertainment

- What kinds of films are popular in your country?
- Why do some people prefer going to the cinema to watching films at home?
- Do you think people will continue going to the cinema in the future?

The Cinema Industry

- Why do you think some countries organise film festivals?
- Which films are more popular in your country: locally made or foreign films?
- Are foreign films in your country usually dubbed, or shown in the original language?
- Do you think governments should support national film industries?

Practice Section 3

Part 1 (4–5 minutes)

In this part, the examiner will ask you 2–3 general questions about yourself:

- Do you live in a city or a town?
- Is it a good place to live for young people?
- Do you like watching television? What kinds of TV programmes did you like to watch when you were a child?
- Do you play any sports? Which one(s)?

Part 2 (3–4 minutes)

The examiner will give you a card topic, a pencil and some paper. You will be given one minute to prepare what you are going to say. You can make notes if you wish to plan your answer. Then the examiner will ask you to speak about the topic for one to two minutes.

Describe a skill (for example, driving, speed reading) you have learned successfully.

You should say:

- **what skill you have learned**
- **why you learned it**
- **who helped you learn it**

and explain what helped you to become good at the skill.

After your talk, the examiner will ask you one or two brief questions about the topic.

- Do you know anyone else who is good at this skill?
- Could you teach this skill to anyone else?

Part 3 (4–5 minutes)

In this part, the examiner will ask you 2–3 general questions related to the topic in Part 2:

Skills and Everyday Life

- Can you compare the skills that are important nowadays with the skills that were important 20 or 30 years ago?
- What skills are valued most in your country?
- What kind of skills might be important in the future?

Skills and Training

- What qualities does a good trainer need to have?
- Why do many companies invest a lot of money in training?
- Do you think schools and universities prepare young people well for future employment?

MODEL ANSWERS FOR PRACTICE SECTIONS

PRACTICE SECTION 1 MODEL ANSWERS

Part 1

Examiner: Hello, my name is …. Can you tell me your name, please?

Candidate: My name is ….

Examiner: Can you show me your I.D., please? Thank you.

Examiner: First, I'd like to ask you a few general questions about yourself. Where do you live?

Candidate: I live in a small town called X, to the north-west of this city, about a 20-minute drive from here.

Examiner: Do you work or study? Where do you work? / Where do you study?

Candidate: I'm studying medicine at the moment, at X university. It's a six-year degree course, and I'm in my third year at the moment.

Examiner: What do you like doing in your free time? Do you have any hobbies?

Candidate: I don't have much free time these days. It's a busy time of the year, but when I do get a free minute to myself, I like to pick up a book or a magazine.

Examiner: Do you cook? How often do you cook?

Candidate: Hmm … I may be able to fry an egg if I'm starving, but no, I don't cook much. I usually go out to restaurants and pubs or get a take-away.

Examiner: Thank you!

Part 2

Examiner: Now in this part, you need to talk about a topic for one minute. You can take a minute to make some notes before you speak. Here is a pencil and some paper for you, and the topic card. I would like you to talk about a city or a town you have enjoyed visiting.

(Candidate makes notes)

Examiner: Now, you have one minute to talk about the topic. I will tell you when to stop.

Candidate: The city I enjoyed visiting is X. I've been there several times. I have a very close friend who lives there, you see, so I try to visit the city every year or so. I was last there in December. There's a lot to do there, lots of museums and the old town, which is a great place if you like that kind of architecture. The night life is really good, too; there are all sorts of music venues, like little jazz bars, all over the city. This time I stayed at my friend's flat for five days. I only spent two days with my friend—he had to go away on business the day after I arrived, so I was left to explore the city on my own. The weather was not that great, but that didn't stop me from going out and enjoying myself. I went out every night and met lots o… interesting people, and even made a couple of new friends. I don't speak the local language, but people are so friendly and easy- going there. When I got lost downtown, a nice young couple helped me find my way back to the flat.

Examiner: Thank you. Would you like to visit the place again?

Candidate: Definitely! I'm going there again this August.

Part 3

Examiner: Now in this part, I would like to ask you a few more general questions about the topic you've talked about. Do people travel more nowadays than they used to in the past?

Candidate: I think so. Travel has become much cheaper and faster than it used to be, say, 20 years ago. Nowadays you can get really cheap tickets from one of those budget airlines and in a few hours be in a different country or even on a different continent. In the past, it might have taken days or even months to travel the same distance. The tourism industry is huge and there is hardly any place left on the planet which you can't get to. Even in this city, which is not a typical tourist destination, you can see lots of tourists, especially in summer.

Examiner: What can one learn from travelling to other countries?

Candidate: Well, lots of things, really. Different cultures, customs and traditions for example. Many people travel abroad to learn a foreign language, which can be much more exciting than learning from books. Those who enjoy visiting museums and galleries can learn a lot about the history and art of the country they are visiting. I personally like to visit parks and green places, and especially places like botanical gardens and zoos, to learn a bit about plant and animal life.

Examiner: What positive or negative effects does tourism have on a local economy?

Candidate: I think generally tourism is very beneficial for local economies as it creates many jobs for local people. Tourists travel with cash which they are ready to spend wherever they travel. There are some negative effects, though. For example, travelling thousands of miles in an airplane to get to a place where you want to spend only a few days is not exactly good for the environment. Also large numbers of visitors can have a huge impact on the local environment, especially in places like national parks. It's true that sustainable tourism is growing, but it is doing so at such a fast pace that it will stop becoming sustainable.

Examiner: Thank you. That's the end of the test.

Practice Section 2 Model Answers

Part 1

Examiner: Hello, my name is …. Can you tell me your name, please?

Candidate: My name is ….

Examiner: Can you show me your I.D., please? Thank you.

Examiner: First, I'd like to ask you a few general questions about yourself. Do you live in a house or a flat?

Candidate: I live in a small rented flat.

Examiner: How long have you lived there?

Candidate: Not long. I moved in there two months ago.

Examiner: Can you briefly describe the flat?

Candidate: Well, it's a small, two-bedroom place, but it's got a nice view of the mountains, and it has a small terrace, which I think is the best thing about it. I'm sharing it with my brother at the moment, but he's planning to find a place of his own next year. The rent is a bit high, but it's not far from where I work, so I don't spend hours commuting every day.

Examiner: Now let's talk about shopping. Do you like shopping?

Candidate: I do, but only for certain things, like clothes or gadgets or books. Most things, except food, I buy online nowadays, from the comfort of my home. I hate food shopping, though. I find it really boring having to buy the same things every time I go to the supermarket.

Examiner: Now let's move on to talk about music. Do you listen to music? What kind of music do you listen to?

Candidate: I listen to music every day. I've got a large collection of old LPs I got from my dad. That's really how I first got interested in music. I listen to all sorts of music. My MP3 player is full of jazz, rock, folk and other sorts of music, but I also like to listen to classical music. I go out to listen to live music whenever I can. In fact, I prefer listening to live rather than recorded music. It's a totally different experience to listen and watch someone play.

Part 2

Examiner: Now in this part, you should talk about a topic for one minute. You can take a minute to make some notes before you speak. Here is a pencil and some paper for you, and the topic card. I would like you to describe a film you saw and really liked.

(Candidate makes notes)

Examiner: Now, you have one minute to talk about the topic. I will tell you when to stop.

Candidate: I have lots of favourite films I like, but I think the best film of all time is X. A friend of mine recommended it to me last year. In fact we watched it together at her place, which was great as I don't like going to the cinema much. It was a film about a boy who was growing up in a small town, about his friends, dreams and problems. I liked it because the plot was quite simple, but it was very interesting. His best friend was a bird—I think it was a hawk or something like that. He found the bird dying in an old barn and nursed it back to health. He got very emotionally attached to the bird, but had to let it go once it recovered. I really liked the photography. There wasn't much dialogue in the film, but it was never boring. It's not really the kind of film I would have picked up in a store, and I would never have watched it if my friend hadn't recommended it to me.

Examiner: Would you like to see the film again?

Candidate: I have it on DVD and actually have seen it a couple of times since then. It really is one of those films worth watching more than once.

Part 3

Examiner:	Now in this part I would like you to ask a few more general questions about the topic you've talked about. What kinds of films are popular in your country?
Candidate:	Well, I guess like anywhere else, Hollywood blockbusters are what most people see. Independent films are also popular, but not as popular as Hollywood movies. There are very few films made locally, so national films are not that big in this country.
Examiner:	Why do you think some people prefer going to the cinema to watching films at home?
Candidate:	I personally like watching films at home. I can't stand it when someone next to me is making a noise eating popcorn, or when a phone goes off in the audience. People who choose to go out and see a movie in a cinema just want a different kind of experience. For them going to see a movie is an event, a change from home. Some people say that the quality of image and sound is much better in the cinema than at home, but I think it matters less now than it used to as many home entertainment systems nowadays can produce just as good a picture and sound.
Examiner:	Do you think people will continue going to the cinema in the future?
Candidate:	Hmm… it's hard to tell, but I think they will. As I said, for many cinema goers going to movies is a social event. They won't want to give it up and stay in to watch a movie. But you never know—technology might be developed which will make it possible to bring a true cinema experience to people's homes.
Examiner:	Thank you. That's the end of the test.

Practice Section 3 Model Answers

Part 1

Examiner: Hello, my name is …. Can you tell me your name, please?

Candidate: My name is ….

Examiner: Can you show me your I.D., please? Thank you.

Examiner: First, I'd like to ask you a few general questions about yourself. Do you live in a city, a town or in the country?

Candidate: I live in a small village not far from this city, about a 30-minute drive from here.

Examiner: Is it a good place to live for young people?

Candidate: I don't think so. There aren't many places to go out to, just one bar and a pier which has got some shops and a cinema. There isn't much night life there. Most young people move to the city once they finish school. I liked growing up there, though, and I went back when I finished my university degree. It's a great place for families with kids, but not if you're young and like going out often.

Examiner: Now, let's talk about television. Do you like watching television?

Candidate: I don't watch TV that much, really. I prefer to pick up a book. I do watch DVDs every now and then, though.

Examiner: What kind of TV programmes did you like to watch when you were a child?

Candidate: I liked programmes about nature—animals and plants, that sort of thing. I still do, but I don't watch them as often as I would like to. They're very informative, especially for kids.

Examiner: Now, let's talk about sports. Do you play any sports? Which ones?

Candidate: No, I don't. I'm terrible at sports. I've always been bad at sports; I guess it's got something to do with my poor eyesight. I'm simply hopeless at any kind of ball sport. It doesn't bother me much, though. I like watching sports, especially winter sports.

Part 2

Examiner: Now in this part, you should talk about a topic for one minute. You can take a minute to make some notes before you speak. Here is a pencil and some paper for you, and the topic card. I would like you to describe a skill, for example, driving, speed reading, or any other skill you have learned successfully.

(Candidate makes notes)

Examiner: Now, you have one minute to talk about the topic. I will tell you when to stop.

Candidate: I'll talk about driving, which I think is the most important skill I've learnt. I've been driving for about ten years now, and I learnt how to drive when I was 16. As I've told you, I lived and grew up in a small village not far from here, and you need a car to go anywhere, so it was essential to drive if you didn't want to feel isolated. My father taught me how to drive, but I didn't get a driving license until I was 20. I also failed my first driving test, and had to do a course with a driving instructor to learn how to drive properly in the city. I've had a car for over six years and I drive every day, but I think it was the formal course and the driving test I had to do that helped me become a good driver.

Examiner: Could you teach this skill to anyone else?

Candidate: I actually have. I've taught my sister to drive.

Part 3

Examiner: Now in this part, I would like to ask you a few more general questions about the topic you've talked about. What qualities does a good trainer need to have?

Candidate: Hmm… let me think…. Well, I suppose one of the most important qualities is to be able to explain and to be patient if one doesn't get it the first or even the tenth time. Another important characteristic is to like helping people learn. These are the most important qualities, in my opinion.

Examiner: Why do you think many companies invest a lot of money in training?

Candidate: Well, I think those companies that want to stay competitive need to invest in training their staff. Businesses are changing so fast nowadays that it's essential to provide employees with the training necessary for them to do their jobs efficiently. Another reason might be that people like to feel valued, and giving them training is one way for a company to show that. The company I work for invests a lot in training, and I see it as one of the major benefits I receive, as it will help me become more employable in the future should I choose to change jobs.

Examiner: Do you think schools and universities prepare young people well for future employment?

Candidate: I don't think so. In most schools and universities, the students' heads are crammed with useless information which helps them pass a test or an exam. I believe people start learning when they leave school and start working. I'm not saying theoretical knowledge isn't important—I'm just saying that a lot of what kids are taught at school won't be very useful for them in the future. There are vocational schools and colleges, however, where young people learn skills for a specific job, for example, welding or carpentry. These do prepare young people for future employment, in my opinion.

Examiner: Thank you. That's the end of the test.

IELTS

PART 3:

PRACTICE TESTS

Please note that the Listening and Speaking modules are the same for both the Academic and General Training Practice Tests. Please use tracks 5 – 8 on the CD for the Listening module, as indicated on the tests.

LISTENING ANSWER SHEET

KAPLAN

PENCIL must be used to complete this sheet

Centre number:

Please write your **name** below,

then write your six digit Candidate number in the boxes
and shade the number in the grid on the right in **PENCIL**.

1 2 3 4 5 6 7 8 9
1 2 3 4 5 6 7 8 9
1 2 3 4 5 6 7 8 9
1 2 3 4 5 6 7 8 9
1 2 3 4 5 6 7 8 9
1 2 3 4 5 6 7 8 9

Test date (shade ONE box for the day, ONE box for the month and ONE box for the year):

Day: 01 02 03 04 05 06 07 08 09 10 11 12 13 14 15 16 17 18 19 20 21 22 23 24 25 26 27 28 29 30 31

Month: 01 02 03 04 05 06 07 08 09 10 11 12   Last 2 digits of the **Year:** 01 02 03 04 05 06 07 08 09

IELTS Listening Answer Sheet

1		21	
2		22	
3		23	
4		24	
5		25	
6		26	
7		27	
8		28	
9		29	
10		30	
11		31	
12		32	
13		33	
14		34	
15		35	
16		36	
17		37	
18		38	
19		39	
20		40	

Checker's Initials   Marker's Initials   Band Score   Listening Total

KAPLAN

READING ANSWER SHEET

KAPLAN

Are you: Female? ⊐ Male? ⊐

Your first language code: ▶ 1 2 3 4 5 6 7 8 9
▶ 1 2 3 4 5 6 7 8 9
▶ 1 2 3 4 5 6 7 8 9

IELTS Reading Answer Sheet

Module taken (shade ONE box): Academic ⊐ General Training ⊐

1		1	21		1
2		2	22		2
3		3	23		3
4		4	24		4
5		5	25		5
6		6	26		6
7		7	27		7
8		8	28		8
9		9	29		9
10		10	30		10
11		11	31		11
12		12	32		12
13		13	33		13
14		14	34		14
15		15	35		15
16		16	36		16
17		17	37		17
18		18	38		18
19		19	39		19
20		20	40		20

| Checker's Initials | | Marker's Initials | | Band Score | | Reading Total | |

WRITING ANSWER SHEET

KAPLAN

- I -

WRITING ANSWER SHEET

Candidate Name: ....

Candidate Number: ....

Centre Name: ....

Date: ....

Module: ACADEMIC [ ]   GENERAL TRAINING [ ]   (Tick as appropiate)

TASK I

EXAMINER'S USE ONLY

EXAMINER 2 NUMBER: ....

CANDIDATE NUMBER: ....   EXAMINER I NUMBER: ....

KAPLAN

KAPLAN

- 2 -

_____

_____

_____

_____

_____

_____

_____

_____

_____

_____

_____

_____

_____

_____

_____

_____

_____

_____

_____

_____

EXAMINER'S USE ONLY

EXAMINER 2 TASK 1

TA		CC		LR		GRA	

UNDERLENGTH		NO OF WORDS		PENALTY	
OFF-TOPIC		MEMORIZED		ILLEGIBLE	

EXAMINER 1 TASK 1

TA		CC		LR		GRA	

UNDERLENGTH		NO OF WORDS		PENALTY	
OFF-TOPIC		MEMORIZED		ILLEGIBLE	

TASK 2

- 3 -

KAPLAN

EXAMINER'S USE ONLY

KAPLAN

- 4 -

EXAMINER'S USE ONLY

EXAMINER 2 TASK 2

TA		CC		LR		GRA	

UNDERLENGTH		NO OF WORDS		PENALTY	
OFF-TOPIC		MEMORIZED		ILLEGIBLE	

EXAMINER 1 TASK 2

TA		CC		LR		GRA	

UNDERLENGTH		NO OF WORDS		PENALTY	
OFF-TOPIC		MEMORIZED		ILLEGIBLE	

ACADEMIC PRACTICE TEST

🎧 ACADEMIC LISTENING MODULE

TIME Approx. 30 minutes + transfer time

Track 5
on CD

Section 1	Questions 1 – 10

Questions 1 – 4

*Complete the notes below. Write NO MORE THAN THREE WORDS AND/OR A NUMBER
for each answer.*

Write your answers in boxes 1-4 on your answer sheet.

NOTES ON COURSES AVAILABLE

Example: *Answer:*

Number of language courses per week   10   ☐

Languages

- Modern European Languages: French, Spanish, German, Dutch, Polish
- Ancient Languages: Latin and **1** .... *acieng* Greek
- Asian Languages: Hindi and **2** .... *Mangali* PELGALI

Cost £25.00 per person per term

Notes: Bulk booking (more than two courses for **3** ...two... terms) *10% discount.*

To reserve a place in a language class, telephone Mary Jones on extension
4 .... 06.94 / 6994 *after 6pm*

KAPLAN

Questions 5 – 10

Complete the table and information below. Write NO MORE THAN THREE WORDS AND/OR A NUMBER for each answer.

Write your answers in boxes **5-10** *on your answer sheet.*

Monthly Computer Courses

Date	Subject	Places available	Cost per person
1st February	5 ...Data basic	24	£40.00
March	Excel	6 ....4.slots only	£45.00
April	Outlook	19	7 £ 60
3rd 8 ...June	Word	9 ......16 vaccancies c	£55.00

To book a place on a computer course, call Mrs Jones before 10 ......6 pm.

Section 2   **Questions 11 – 20**

(Track 6
on CD)

Questions 11 – 17

Complete this summary of the welcoming speech. Write NO MORE THAN THREE WORDS OR A NUMBER for each answer.

Write your answers in boxes 11-17 on your answer sheet.

—3

Dear Joe,

You missed the Welcome meeting. We were greeted by the Principal of Donleavy
11 ..*University*.. who explained how the University has 12 ..*3 science*.. campuses.
He told us where all the important buildings on this campus are and also explained which
subjects are studied on the other two. The principal's
13 ..*office*.. is on our campus.

We must carry our 14 ..*ID passes*.. to get into the campus. The University shop sells 15
..*stationery* and *native*.. and is next to the cafeteria.

You need to use your 16 ..*ID passes*.. when you buy things in both of them. There will
be a lot of building work because they are building a 17 ..*security season*.. during this term.

Regards,

Rebecca

Questions 18 – 20

Complete the labels on the buildings on the map. Write NO MORE THAN THREE WORDS OR A NUMBER for each answer.

Write your answers in boxes **18-20** *on your answer sheet.*

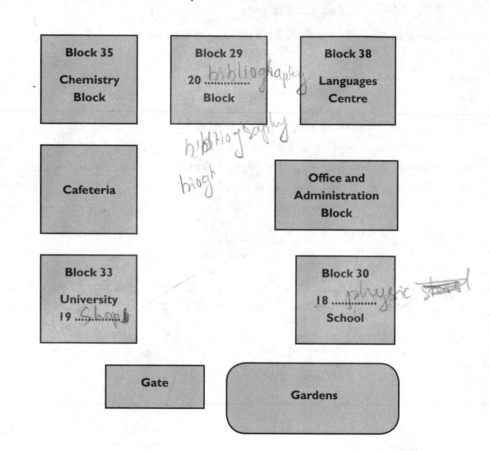

Section 3   **Questions 21 – 30**

Track 7
on CD

Choose the correct letter **A**, **B** *or* **C**.

Write your answers in boxes **21-30** *on your answer sheet.*

21   Bill was ill. What was wrong?

    A   A cold ✗

    B   A food allergy

    (C)   A severe pain in his head

22   Bill and Sarah

    A   live near each other.

    (B)   have never worked on a project together. ✗

    C   have plans for later that evening.

23   Bill and Sarah have to

    A   research and write a survey questionnaire.

    (B)   ask shopkeepers questions.

    C   submit their project via the Internet.

24   What does Sarah want Bill to do?

    A   Visit the library

    (B)   Write a list of questions

    C   Use a computer

25   Which of the following items will be included in Bill and Sarah's research?

    (A)   Deodorants and cosmetics

    B   Electrical goods

    C   Food and clothing

26   With what aspect of the project does Bill express concern?

    A   Meeting the project's timeline

    (B)   Invading people's privacy

    C   Finding enough reference material

27   What does Bill plan to do for the rest of the day?

    A   Review the previous week's classes.

    (B)   Prepare notes for his next meeting with Sarah.

    C   Find people to participate in the research.

28   What does Sarah do for Bill?

    A   Helps him catch up on the notes

    B   Gives him a copy of her notes

    C   Promises to help him study

29   What does Sarah have to do at the library?

    A   Research

    B   Meet Bill

    C   Collect some books

30   Where do Bill and Sarah agree to meet the next day?

    A   In the library

    B   In class

    C   In the laboratory

Track 8
on CD

Section 4   **Questions 31 – 40**

Questions 31 – 32

Choose the correct letter **A**, **B** *or* **C**.

Write your answers in boxes **31-32** *on your answer sheet.*

31   Who is giving this talk?

    A   An artist

    B   An art critic

    C   A curator

32   Why did the speaker choose to speak about Joan Miró?

    A   Because a new work by Miró was recently added to the gallery.

    B   Because he thought Miró would appeal to people with different tastes.

    C   Because he felt everyone would be familiar with Joan Miró's art.

Questions 33 – 35

Which **three** *features below are mentioned by the speaker as characteristic of Joan Miró's art? Choose* **THREE** *letters,* **A-G***.*

Write your answers in boxes **33-35** *on your answer sheet.*

A   Themes from Spanish history

B   The use of primary colors

C   Influence of surrealism

D   Complex geometric forms

E   Large paintings

F   Equal number of sculptures and paintings

G   Birds and trees

Questions 36 – 40

*Complete this table with information from the listening. Write ONE OR TWO WORDS OR
A NUMBER in the box.*

Write your answers in boxes **36-40** *on your answer sheet.*

THREE OF MIRÓ'S GREAT WORKS

TITLE	DATE	LOCATION	DETAILS
"Woman and 36 *bird* "	1982	A 37 *Paris* in Barcelona.	Tall sculpture, covered in 38 *material* *mosaic*
"Woman"	39 *1976*	National Gallery of Art, Washington	Large canvas, bright colours
"Seated Woman II"	1939	Guggenheim Museum, New York	Painted when Miró was influenced by the 40 *civil war* in Spain.

KAPLAN

12ʰ30
20:30

ACADEMIC READING MODULE

READING PASSAGE 1

You should spend about 20 minutes on **Questions 1 – 13**, *which are based on Reading Passage 1 below.*

Gender selection—the choosing of a baby's gender prior to birth—occurs in many parts of the world. In China and India, for example, a baby's gender is considered to be of vital importance to the family, and male babies are often preferred over females for cultural reasons. In western countries as well, there are many reasons why a family might want to choose a baby's sex. Often parents wish to have a mix of both boys and girls in the family. There are also health reasons for gender selection: many diseases affect children of only one sex and a family that is susceptible to these diseases may wish to choose a baby's gender to avoid having an affected child.

This demand for gender choice for parents has led scientists worldwide to investigate gender selection prior to conception. Conventional wisdom states that the father's sperm is the main determinant of the child's gender, but recent research has begun to reveal a number of other possible determining factors.

Elissa Cameron's 2007 research at the African University of Pretoria investigated the effects of diet on sex ratios at birth. In one experiment, she changed the blood sugar level of female mice prior to conception by putting a chemical in the animals' water. Mice that received the additive saw their blood sugar levels fall from 6.47 to 5.24 millimols/litre. A separate control group of mice received pure water, without the additive. After a few days, the two groups of mice were allowed to mate. In the control group, 41% of the mice were born female, as compared to 47% in the group that received the additive—a disparity that Dr Cameron ascribed to the differences in the mothers' blood sugar levels.

Interestingly, the idea that blood sugar levels affect a baby's sex follows traditional wisdom. It has long been believed that mothers should eat more red meat and salty foods—which raise blood sugar for a long period—if they want to have a boy; they are advised to eat chocolates and sweets—which raise blood sugar levels for a short time only—if they want a girl.

Another researcher in this field, Fiona Matthews of the University of Exeter, England, has come up with further evidence in support of the effect of diet on the sex of the unborn child. Her study followed 740 pregnant women who kept detailed records of their diets before conception. Her study found that mothers who consumed high-energy foods prior to conception were slightly more likely to have boys. The food with the greatest effect seemed to be breakfast cereals, which tend to be high in energy and often high in sodium content as well. Among women eating cereals on a daily basis, 59% had boys, compared with 43% of women who ate less than one bowl of breakfast cereal per week. These results are said to echo those seen in other animals, for example horses and cows, which statistically bear more males when well-fed.

The eating habits of women in rich western countries could explain the slight fall in male births that has been reported over the past several years. In the UK, male births are falling by 1 per 1,000 births per year. This could be ascribed to the decline in the number of adults and adolescent girls eating breakfast on a regular basis. In addition, the popularity of low-calorie diets for females of child-bearing age could also be a factor contributing to the reduction in male births.

The recent decline in male births in western countries appears to make sense if one looks at it from an evolutionary standpoint. Historically, more boys tend to be born in times of food plenty, while females tend to be born in times of scarcity. One explanation is that when food is scarce, it is better for the survival of the species for female children to be born—as one male can father offspring by many females. Lower-calorie diets among western women could be biologically echoing the effects of scarcity—hence, the decline in male births.

So what can we conclude from this complicated picture? If you would like to have a son, it might be a good idea to eat a breakfast that includes cereal. On the other hand, if you would prefer to give birth to a daughter, then cut out breakfast and continue a weight reduction diet at least until after conception.

Questions 1 – 8

Do the following statements agree with the information given in Reading Passage 1?

In boxes **1-8** on your answer sheet, write

TRUE	if the statement agrees with the information
FALSE	if the statement contradicts the information
NOT GIVEN	if there is no information on this

1   Mothers in India eat cereals for breakfast so that they will have male babies.

2   New drugs have been developed that allow parents to choose the sex of their child.

3   People used to think that the father was responsible for the sex of the baby.

4   Elissa Cameron used both humans and mice in her research.

5   The majority of research on gender selection is happening in Europe.

6   People in the United Kingdom often do not eat breakfast.

7   Some people think that drinking tea has an effect on the sex of a baby.

8   High-calorie diets have been shown to increase the likelihood of female births.

KAPLAN

Questions 9 – 13

*Complete each sentence with the correct ending, **A-K**, below.*

*Write the correct letter, **A-K**, in boxes **9-13** on your answer sheet.*

9   Elissa Cameron   A

10   In western countries, gender selection   G

11   Fiona Matthews   C

12   Evolution seems to support   D

13   Eating breakfast cereal on a daily basis   K

A artificially decreased the blood sugar levels of mice.

B is often based on cultural preferences.

C asked patients to write down everything that they ate and when they ate it.

D the influence of food scarcity upon sex ratios at birth.

E that adding sodium to food affects the sex of a baby.

F is an American scientist.

G sometimes occurs for health reasons.

H an equal balance between male and female children.

I conducted research on horses and cows.

J is more common in the UK than in other western countries.

K seems to increase the likelihood of male births.

Question 14

*Choose the correct letter, **A, B, C, D** or **E**.*

*Write your answer in box **14** on your answer sheet.*

Which of the following is the most suitable title for Reading Passage 1?

A   Eating Cereal is Good for Pregnant Women

B   Research Says Mice Make Better Mothers

C   Diet May Influence the Sex of Your Baby

D   Asian Research Influences Western Medicine

E   Gender Selection Research Sparks Scientific Debate

12ᵏ 50

READING PASSAGE 2

You should spend about 20 minutes on **Questions 15 – 27**, *which are based on Reading Passage 2 below.*

The Disease Multiple Sclerosis

A Multiple Sclerosis (MS) is a disease in which the patient's immune system attacks the central nervous system. This can lead to numerous physical and mental symptoms, as the disease affects the transmission of electrical signals between the body and the brain. However, the human body, being a flexible, adaptable system, can compensate for some level of damage, so a person with MS can look and feel fine even though the disease is present.

B MS patients can have one of two main varieties of the disease: the relapsing form and the primary progressive form. In the relapsing form, the disease progresses in a series of jumps; at times it is in remission, which means that a person's normal functions return for a period of time before the system goes into relapse and the disease again becomes more active. This is the most common form of MS; 80-90% of people have this form of the disease when they are first diagnosed. The relapse–remission cycle can continue for many years. Eventually, however, loss of physical and cognitive functions starts to take place and the remissions become less frequent.

C In the primary progressive form of MS, there are no remissions and a continual but steady loss of physical and cognitive functions takes place. This condition affects about 10-15% of sufferers at diagnosis.

D The expected course of the disease, or prognosis, depends on many variables: the subtype of the disease, the patient's individual characteristics and the initial symptoms. Life expectancy of patients, however, is often nearly the same as that of an unaffected person—provided that a reasonable standard of care is received. In some cases a near-normal life span is possible.

E The cause of the disease is unclear; it seems that some people have a genetic susceptibility, which is triggered by some unknown environmental factor. Onset of the disease usually occurs in young adults between the ages of 20 and 40. It is more common in women than men; however, it has also been diagnosed in young children and in elderly people.

F Hereditary factors have been seen to have some relevance. Studies of identical twins have shown that if one twin has the disease, then it is likely that the other twin will develop it. In addition, it is important to realise that close relatives of patients have a higher chance of developing the disease than people without a relative who has MS.

G   Where people live can be seen to have a clear effect, as MS does not occur as frequently in every country. It commonly affects Caucasian people, particularly in North America, Europe and Australia. It has been recognised that MS is more common the further the country is away from the equator, and the incidence of MS is generally much higher in northern countries with temperate climates than in warmer southern countries.

H   Three things, which do not normally occur in healthy people, happen to people who have MS. First, tiny patches of inflammation occur in the brain or spinal chord. Second, the protective coating around the axons, or nerve fibres, in the body starts to deteriorate. Third, the axons themselves become damaged or destroyed. This can lead to a wide range of symptoms in the patient, depending on where the affected axons are located.

I   A common symptom of MS is blurred vision, caused by inflammation of the optic nerve. Another sign is loss of muscle tone in arms and legs; this is when control of muscle movement, or strength in the arms or legs, can be lost. Sense of touch can be lost, so that the body is unable to feel heat or cold, or the sufferer experiences temperature inappropriately, that is, feeling heat when it is cold and vice versa. Balance can also be affected; some people may eventually have to resort to a wheel-chair, either on a permanent or temporary basis. The course of the disease varies from person to person.

J   A diagnosis of MS is often confirmed by the use of a Magnetic Resonance Imaging (MRI) scan, which can show defects in the brain and spinal chord. Once diagnosed, MS is a lifelong disease; no cure exists, although a number of medical treatments have been shown to reduce relapses and slow the progression of the disease. It is important that patients with the disease are diagnosed early, so that treatment, which can slow the disease, can be started early.

Questions 15 – 19

Reading passage 2 has 10 paragraphs labelled **A-J**.

Which paragraph contains the following information?

Write the correct letters, **A-J**, *in boxes* **15-19** *on your answer sheet.*

NB   *You may use any letter more than once.*

15   The main types of the disease   B

16   Loss of the sense of feeling   I

17   The progress of the disease   C

18   Treatments for the disease   J

19   The effects of geography   G

Questions 20 – 27

Complete the table below.

Choose NO MORE THAN THREE WORDS from the passage for each answer.

Write your answers in boxes 20-27 on your answer sheet.

Main Types of 20 ...~~relapsing~~ form (multiple sclerosis	
21 ...relapsing form 80-90% of sufferers	Primary Progressive Form 22 ...10-15 percent... of patients
Causes are unclear	
23 ...Genetic sus:susceptibility 24 ...Caucasian...people are more often affected than other races. There is a higher incidence where the weather is 25 ...temperate (colder)	Hereditary If one 26 ...twin... is affected the other is likely to develop MS.

Three effects of MS		
Inflammation in the brain and/or 27 ...Spinal cord	Coating of nerve fibres damaged	Axons themselves damaged.

READING PASSAGE 3

You should spend about 20 minutes on **Questions 27 – 40**, *which are based on Reading Passage 3 below.*

Surge Protection

With more and more devices connecting to the world's electrical networks, protecting electrical systems and devices from power surges—also known as *distribution overcurrent*—has become more important than ever. Without adequate overcurrent protection, interruptions to electrical service can have catastrophic effects on individuals, cities and entire nations.

In a normal electrical system, customers are supplied with a steady electrical current—a predetermined voltage necessary to safely operate all electrical equipment connected to that system. This steady electrical supply is subject to minimal variations—variations that are imperceptible to the consumer and do not normally harm electrical devices. An overload current is any surge that exceeds the variances of this normal operating current. The higher the overcurrent, the more potential it has to damage electrical devices. One of the most important principles of overcurrent protection, therefore, is that the higher the magnitude of the overload current, the faster the overcurrent must be interrupted.

How do overcurrents occur? Most overcurrents are temporary and harmless, caused when motors start up or transformers are energised. Such things as defective motors, overloaded equipment or too many loads on one circuit, however, can cause harmful, sustained overcurrents, which must be shut off quickly to avoid damaging the entire distribution system. An inadequately protected system can cause damage ranging from electrical shocks to people coming in contact with electrical equipment, to fires caused by the thermal ignition of electrical materials on the overloaded circuit.

Electrical storms and lightning are among the biggest causes of major distribution overcurrent worldwide. In the United States alone, 67 people are killed every year by these types of storms (including those killed by falling trees and power lines—not only surges). The intense current of a lightning discharge creates a fleeting, but very strong, magnetic field. A single lightning strike can produce up to a billion volts of electricity. If lightning strikes a house, it can easily destroy all the electrical equipment inside, and damage the distribution system to which that house is connected.

To protect people and devices adequately, overcurrent protection needs to be *sensitive*, *selective*, *fast* and *reliable*. In the interest of conservation, most power systems generate different loads at different times of the day; overcurrent protection must therefore be *sensitive* enough to operate under conditions of both minimum and maximum power generation. It also needs to be *selective* so that it can differentiate between conditions that require immediate action and those where limited action is required; in other words, it should shut down the minimum number of devices to avoid disrupting the rest of the electrical system. Overcurrent protection also needs to be *fast*; it should be able to quickly disconnect undamaged equipment from the area of overcurrent and thus prevent the spread of the fault. Of course, the most basic requirement of protective equipment is that it is *reliable*, performing correctly wherever and whenever it is needed.

When an overcurrent occurs at a major electricity supply point such as a power station, the resulting surge, if it is not checked, can damage the entire distribution system. Like a flooding river—which breaks its banks and floods smaller rivers, which in turn flood streets and houses—the extra voltage courses through the network of wires and devices that comprise the distribution system, until it discharges its excessive energy into the earth. This is why each piece of equipment within the electricity manufacturing and distribution system must be protected by a *grounding* or *earthing* mechanism—the grounding mechanism allows the excess electricity to be discharged into the earth directly, instead of passing it further down the distribution system.

Within the distribution system, surge protection is provided by overcurrent relays. Relays are simply switches that open and close under the control of another electrical circuit; an overcurrent relay is a specific type of relay that operates only when the voltage on a power line exceeds a predetermined level. If the source of an overcurrent is nearby, the overcurrent relay shuts off instantaneously. One danger, however, is that when one electrical circuit shuts down, the electricity may be rerouted through adjacent circuits, causing them to become overloaded. At its most extreme, this can lead to the 'blackout' of an entire electrical network. To protect against this, overcurrent relays have a time-delay response; when the source of an overcurrent is far away, the overcurrent relays delay slightly before shutting down—thereby allowing some of the current through to the next circuit, so that no single circuit becomes overloaded. An additional benefit of this system is that when power surges do occur, engineers are able to use these time delay sequences to calculate the source of the fault.

Fuses and circuit breakers are the normal overcurrent protection devices found in private homes. Both devices operate similarly: they allow the passage of normal currents, but quickly 'trip', or interrupt, when too much current flows through. Fuses and circuit breakers are normally located in the home's electrical switch box—which takes the main power coming into the house and distributes it to various parts of the home. Beyond this level of home protection, it is also advisable to purchase additional 'tripping' devices for sensitive electrical devices such as computers, telephones and modems. While many electrical devices are equipped with internal surge protection, the value of these devices usually warrants additional protection such as may be gained from purchasing an additional protective device.

The modern world could not exist without reliable electricity generation and distribution. While overcurrents cannot be entirely avoided, it is possible to mitigate their effects by providing adequate protection at every level of the electrical system, from the main power generation stations to the individual home devices we all rely upon in our daily lives.

Questions 28 – 33

Choose the correct letter, **A, B, C** *or* **D**.

Write your answers in boxes **28-33** *on your answer sheet.*

28   In a normal electrical system,

- **A**   voltage differences are usually quite small.
- **B**   overcurrent protection is mainly provided by circuit breakers and fuses.
- **C**   different amounts of electricity are generated at different times of day.
- **D**   some circuits constantly experience a certain level of overcurrent.

29   The writer suggests that most overcurrents.

- **A**   are harmless and temporary.
- **B**   affect all levels of the distribution system.
- **C**   are triggered by electrical storms.
- **D**   can be instantaneously controlled by relays.

30   What does the writer state is the *most basic* requirement of overcurrent protection equipment?

- **A**   Speed
- **B**   Selectivity
- **C**   Sensitivity
- **D**   Reliability

31   The writer suggests that most household electrical devices

- **A**   are adequately protected by the home's electrical switch box.
- **B**   should be protected from overcurrent by additional devices.
- **C**   produce strong magnetic fields that can sometimes cause surges.
- **D**   are designed to shut off after a short time delay.

32   In which of the following circumstances might the shut-down of an   overcurrent relay be delayed?

- **A**   If the source of an overcurrent is nearby
- **B**   If an overcurrent is caused by an electrical storm
- **C**   If an entire electrical network experiences 'blackout'
- **D**   If the source of an overcurrent is far away

33 What is an essential safety requirement for every device in an electrical system?

    A   A grounding mechanism

    B   The ability to shut down quickly

    C   Sensitivity to variances in the electrical system

    D   Internal surge protection

Questions 34 – 40

Do the following statements agree with the information given in Reading Passage 3?

In boxes **34-40** on your answer sheet, write

TRUE	if the statement agrees with the information
FALSE	if the statement contradicts the information
NOT GIVEN	if there is no information on this

34 Effective overcurrent protection systems shut down as few devices as possible.

35 Electricians must use special tools to fit fuses. NG

36 The most common cause of overcurrents is the presence of too many loads on one circuit.

37 Overcurrents course through the entire distribution system unless they are discharged into the earth.

38 Over one hundred people are killed by electrical storms worldwide each year.

39 The effects of overcurrents are magnified when electricity comes in contact with water.

40 All variations in electrical voltage are potentially damaging, and must be prevented.

ACADEMIC WRITING MODULE

WRITING TASK I

You should spend about 20 minutes on this task.

The table below shows the number of Internet users in nine countries in June 2007. It also shows the percentage of the population who use the Internet in these countries, and the percentage of world users that this represents.

Summarise the information by selecting the main features, and making comparisons between countries.

Write at least 150 words.

Country	Internet users, latest data	Penetration (% Population)	% of World Users
United States	210,575,287	69.7%	18.0%
China	162,000,000	12.3%	13.8%
India	42,000,000	3.7%	3.6%
United Kingdom	37,600,000	62.3%	3.2%
France	32,925,953	53.7%	2.8%
Indonesia	20,000,000	8.9%	1.7%
Spain	19,765,033	43.9%	1.7%
Australia	15,085,600	71.9%	1.3%
Philippines	14,000,000	16.0%	1.2%

WRITING TASK 2

You should spend about 40 minutes on this task.

Write about the following topic.

Compare the advantages and disadvantages of three of the following as places where advertisers might place advertisements for cars.

Explain which you think would be the most effective.

- *Cinema*
- *Radio*
- *Billboards*
- *Television*
- *Newspapers*
- *Magazines*

Give reasons for your answer and include any relevant examples from your own experience.

Write at least 250 words.

ACADEMIC SPEAKING MODULE

(10-15 minutes)

PART ONE

Introduction to interview, 4-5 minutes

The examiner will begin by introducing him/herself and checking your identity.

S/he will then ask you some questions about yourself, based on everyday topics.

- Let's talk about the place where you live now.
- Describe the place where you live now.
- Were you born there?
- Do you live on your own or with your family?
- Has the place changed much over the time you have lived there? (How?)

PART TWO

Individual long turn, 3-4 minutes

Candidates' task card
INSTRUCTIONS

Please read the topic below carefully. You will be asked to talk about it for 1 to 2 minutes.

You will have one minute to think about what you're going to say.

You can make some notes to help you if you wish.

> **Describe a musical event you enjoyed attending.**
>
> **You should say:**
>
> - **what the event you attended was**
> - **where it took place**
> - **who was with you**
>
> **and explain why you enjoyed attending the event.**

The examiner may then ask you a couple of brief questions to show that this part of the test is over.

Further questions:

- Do you play music yourself?
- What instruments can you play?
- What kind of music do you most enjoy? What do you like about it?

PART THREE

Two-way discussion, 4-5 minutes

In Part Three the examiner will ask you further questions related to the topic in Part Two. Let's consider listening to music …

- How expensive is it to attend a concert in your country?
- Is it better to listen to live music, or to listen to music on the television or radio? Why is this better?
- Do you think there is too much music available now? Why/Why not?

Finally let's talk about famous musicians…

- Why do you think people are so interested in the personal lives of musicians?
- Is that interest stronger now than in the past?
- What are some of the things that can affect the image and popularity of musicians?

LISTENING ANSWER SHEET

KAPLAN

PENCIL must be used to complete this sheet

Centre number:

Please write your **name** below,

then write your six digit Candidate number in the boxes
and shade the number in the grid on the right in **PENCIL.**

Test date (shade ONE box for the day, ONE box for the month and ONE box for the year):

Day: 01 02 03 04 05 06 07 08 09 10 11 12 13 14 15 16 17 18 19 20 21 22 23 24 25 26 27 28 29 30 31

Month: 01 02 03 04 05 06 07 08 09 10 11 12   Last 2 digits of the **Year:** 01 02 03 04 05 06 07 08 09

IELTS Listening Answer Sheet

#		✓ / ✗	#		✓ / ✗
1		1	21		1
2		2	22		2
3		3	23		3
4		4	24		4
5		5	25		5
6		6	26		6
7		7	27		7
8		8	28		8
9		9	29		9
10		10	30		10
11		11	31		11
12		12	32		12
13		13	33		13
14		14	34		14
15		15	35		15
16		16	36		16
17		17	37		17
18		18	38		18
19		19	39		19
20		20	40		20

Checker's Initials		Marker's Initials		Band Score		Listening Total	

KAPLAN

READING ANSWER SHEET

KAPLAN

Are you: Female? ▭   Male? ▭

Your first language code: ▶ 1 2 3 4 5 6 7 8 9
   ▶ 1 2 3 4 5 6 7 8 9
   ▶ 1 2 3 4 5 6 7 8 9

IELTS Reading Answer Sheet

Module taken (shade ONE box):   Academic ▭   General Training ▭

1		1	21		1
2		2	22		2
3		3	23		3
4		4	24		4
5		5	25		5
6		6	26		6
7		7	27		7
8		8	28		8
9		9	29		9
10		10	30		10
11		11	31		11
12		12	32		12
13		13	33		13
14		14	34		14
15		15	35		15
16		16	36		16
17		17	37		17
18		18	38		18
19		19	39		19
20		20	40		20

Checker's Initials		Marker's Initials		Band Score		Reading Total	

KAPLAN

WRITING ANSWER SHEET

KAPLAN

- 1 -

WRITING ANSWER SHEET

Candidate Name: ....

Candidate Number: ....

Centre Name: ....

Date: ....

Module: ACADEMIC [ ]   GENERAL TRAINING [ ]   (Tick as appropiate)

TASK 1

_____

_____

_____

_____

_____

_____

_____

_____

_____

_____

_____

_____

_____

_____

_____

_____

_____

_____

_____

EXAMINER'S USE ONLY

EXAMINER 2 NUMBER: ....

CANDIDATE NUMBER: ....   EXAMINER 1 NUMBER: ....

KAPLAN

- 2 -

EXAMINER 2 TASK 1

TA		CC		LR		GRA	

UNDERLENGTH		NO OF WORDS		PENALTY	
OFF-TOPIC		MEMORIZED		ILLEGIBLE	

EXAMINER 1 TASK 1

TA		CC		LR		GRA	

UNDERLENGTH		NO OF WORDS		PENALTY	
OFF-TOPIC		MEMORIZED		ILLEGIBLE	

KAPLAN

TASK 2 - 3 - KAPLAN

_____

EXAMINER'S USE ONLY

KAPLAN

- 4 -

(lined answer space)

EXAMINER'S USE ONLY

EXAMINER 2 TASK 2

TA		CC		LR		GRA	

UNDERLENGTH		NO OF WORDS		PENALTY	
OFF-TOPIC		MEMORIZED		ILLEGIBLE	

EXAMINER 1 TASK 2

TA		CC		LR		GRA	

UNDERLENGTH		NO OF WORDS		PENALTY	
OFF-TOPIC		MEMORIZED		ILLEGIBLE	

KAPLAN

GENERAL TRAINING PRACTICE TEST

🎧 GENERAL TRAINING LISTENING MODULE

TIME Approx. 30 minutes + transfer time

| Section I | Questions I – 10 | *Track 5 on CD* |

Questions I – 4

Complete the notes below. Write NO MORE THAN THREE WORDS AND/OR A NUMBER for each answer.

Write your answers in boxes **I-4** *on your answer sheet.*

NOTES ON COURSES AVAILABLE

Example: *Answer:*

Number of language courses per week   10   ☐

Languages

- Modern European Languages: French, Spanish, German, Dutch, Polish
- Ancient Languages: Latin and **I** ....
- Asian Languages: Hindi and **2** ....

Cost £25.00 per person per term

Notes: Bulk booking (more than two courses for **3** .... terms) *10% discount.*

To reserve a place in a language class, telephone Mary Jones on extension

4 ....

Questions 5 – 10

Complete the table and information below. Write NO MORE THAN THREE WORDS AND/OR A NUMBER for each answer.

Write your answers in boxes **5-10** *on your answer sheet.*

Monthly Computer Courses

Date	Subject	Places available	Cost per person
1st February	5	24	£40.00
March	Excel	6 .... only	£45.00
April	Outlook	19	7 £ ....
3rd 8	Word	9	£55.00

To book a place on a computer course, call Mrs Jones before **10** ....

Section 2 **Questions 11 – 20** Track 6 on CD

Questions 11 – 17

Complete this summary of the welcoming speech. Write NO MORE THAN THREE WORDS OR A NUMBER for each answer.

Write your answers in boxes 11-17 on your answer sheet.

Dear Joe,

You missed the Welcome meeting. We were greeted by the Principal of Donleavy 11 ……….................. who explained how the University has 12 ……….................. campuses. He told us where all the important buildings on this campus are and also explained which subjects are studied on the other two. The principal's 13 ……….................. is on our campus.

We must carry our 14 ……….................. to get into the campus. The University shop sells 15 ……….................. and ……….................. and is next to the cafeteria.

You need to use your 16 ……….................. when you buy things in both of them. There will be a lot of building work because they are building a 17……….................. during this term.

Regards,

Rebecca

Questions 18 – 20

Complete the labels on the buildings on the map. Write NO MORE THAN THREE WORDS OR A NUMBER for each answer.

Rio
Bo~

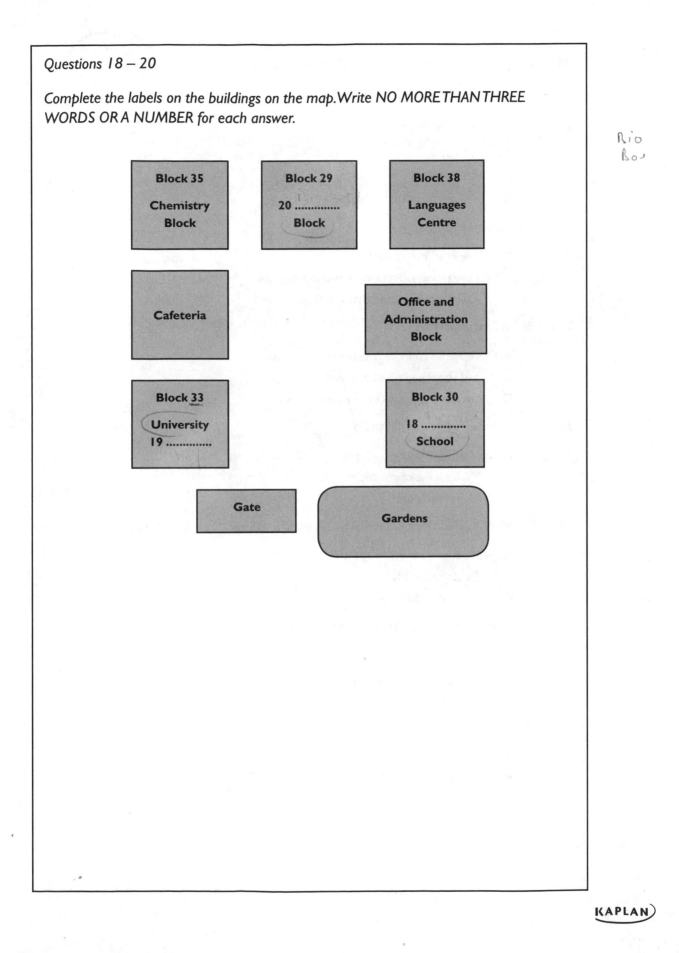

Section 3　　　　　**Questions 21 – 30**

Track 7
on CD

Choose the correct letter, **A**, **B** *or* **C**.

21　Bill was ill. What was wrong?

    A　A cold

    B　A food allergy

    C　A severe pain in his head

22　Bill and Sarah

    A　live near each other.

    B　have never worked on a project together.

    C　have plans for later that evening.

23　Bill and Sarah have to

    A　research and write a survey questionnaire.

    B　ask shopkeepers questions.

    C　submit their project via the Internet.

24　What does Sarah want Bill to do?

    A　Visit the library

    B　Write a list of questions

    C　Use a computer

25　Which of the following items will be included in Bill and Sarah's research?

    A　Deodorants and cosmetics

    B　Electrical goods

    C　Food and clothing

26　With what aspect of the project does Bill express concern?

    A　Meeting the project's timeline

    B　Invading people's privacy

    C　Finding enough reference material

27　What does Bill plan to do for the rest of the day?

    A　Review the previous week's classes.

    B　Prepare notes for his next meeting with Sarah.

    C　Find people to participate in the research.

28   What does Sarah do for Bill?

    A   Helps him catch up on the notes

    B   Gives him a copy of her notes

    C   Promises to help him study

29   What does Sarah have to do at the library?

    A   Research

    B   Meet Bill

    C   Collect some books

30   Where do Bill and Sarah agree to meet the next day?

    A   In the library

    B   In class

    C   In the laboratory

Section 4   **Questions 31 – 40**

Track 8
on CD

Questions 31 – 32

Choose the correct letter **A**, **B** *or* **C.**

31   Who is giving this talk?

     A   An artist

     B   An art critic

     C   A curator

32   Why did the speaker choose to speak about Joan Miró?

     A   Because a new work by Miró was recently added to the gallery.

     B   Because he thought Miró would appeal to people with different tastes.

     C   Because he felt everyone would be familiar with Joan Miró's art.

Questions 33 – 35

Which **three** *features below are mentioned by the speaker as characteristic of Joan Miró's art? Choose* **THREE** *letters,* **A-G**.

A   Themes from Spanish history
B   The use of primary colors
C   Influence of surrealism
D   Complex geometric forms
E   Large paintings
F   Equal number of sculptures and paintings
G   Birds and trees

Questions 36 – 40

Complete this table with information from the listening. Write ONE OR TWO WORDS OR A NUMBER in the box.

*Write your answers in boxes **36-40** on your answer sheet.*

THREE OF MIRÓ'S GREAT WORKS

TITLE	DATE	LOCATION	DETAILS
"Woman and 36 ...."	1982	A 37 .... in Barcelona.	Tall sculpture, covered in 38 ....
"Woman"	39	National Gallery of Art, Washington	Large canvas, bright colours
"Seated Woman II"	1939	Guggenheim Museum, New York	Painted when Miró was influenced by the 40 .... in Spain.

GENERAL TRAINING READING MODULE

TIME One hour

SECTION 1

You should spend about 20 minutes on **Questions 1 – 14**.

Read the text below and answer **Questions 1 – 7**.

First Floor		Second Floor	
Emergency Services		**Opthalmology**	
Reception	101	Reception	200
Treatment Rooms	102-110	Dr Ana Boto	201
Waiting Room	111-113	Dr Jina Williams	202
		Dr Geoff Foreman	203
		Dr Susan Widden	204
		Waiting Room	205
Internal Medicine		**Tropical Diseases**	
Reception	114	Reception	211
Waiting Room	115	Waiting Room	212
Dr Ben Keran	116	Quarantine	213
Dr Janet Goldsmith	117	Dr Viet Nguyen	214
Dr Christopher Sherin	118	Dr Pongsambulnar Cutler	215
Dr Rashmi Pandi	119	Dr Luisa Doyle	216
Dr Mabel Chew	120	Dr Lea Kynaston	217
Dr Donald Tuffy	121		
General Practice		**Heart Disease Unit**	
Reception	122	Reception	221
Dr Mary Garcia	123	Dr David Parker	222
Dr Helena Ho	124	Dr Neil Kennedy	223
Dr Jackie Jimenez	125	Dr Julian Crosby	224
Dr Tania Cherrin	126	Dr Alison Cussons	225
Dr Toshio Nishima	127	Dr Fiona Darby	226
Dr Ross Smith	128	Waiting Room	227
Waiting Room	129		
Services		**Surgical Unit**	
Toilets	130 and 131	Reception	230
Cafeteria	132	Surgeries	231–238
Banking and Telephoning Service	133	Recovery Room	239
Children's Play Room	134	Waiting Room	240
Florist and Gift Shop	140		

Notices

When you arrive at the hospital, please go to *Reception* in the relevant specialty area and register with the receptionist. You will then be shown to the waiting room where you will be asked to wait until your name is called. The waiting time varies according to the number of patients, and we ask for your patience and understanding. The reception staff will be able to give you information regarding how many people are ahead of you, but will not be able to give you an exact time for seeing the doctor.

If you have ten or more people ahead of you, you may wish to leave the waiting room and relax in other areas of the hospital (cafeteria, gardens or children's playroom). In this case, ask the receptionist for a pager; you will be paged when there are fewer people ahead of you. *Please come straight back to the reception area when paged.*

While in the waiting room, please
switch off your mobile phone;
keep noise to a minimum;
refrain from eating and drinking (except water from the coolers provided);
do not smoke;
ensure that children are kept close at all times (you may wish to take them to the playroom).

Any discourteous or aggressive treatment of hospital staff or other patients will be dealt with immediately.

Questions 1 – 6

Read the questions below and write the appropriate room number in **boxes 1-6** *on your answer sheet.*

Which room will you go to when you

1   want a cup of coffee?

2   are waiting to see Dr Kynaston?

3   need treatment in an emergency?

4   want to see a doctor about your heart condition?

5   have bored, noisy children with you?

6   have an appointment with a General Practitioner?

Question 7

Which of these things **can** *you do in the waiting room? Write the words in* **box 7** *on your answer sheet.*

Page a doctor

Drink coffee

Eat snacks

Drink water

Use your phone

Questions 8-14

*Read the accommodation information on this page. Select the best accommodation for each student on the list below and write the correct letter, **A-H**, in boxes **8-14** on your answer sheet.*

*(**NB** There are more offers of accommodation than there are students.)*

Student Accommodation

A	4 students living in 5-bedroom house, looking for one more student to share. We are all serious, hard-working students who don't have much time for fun. We usually work in our rooms or in the library, but we have dinner together most nights. Share cooking and cleaning work.	E	Rex Student Hostel—rooms available for students. Dinner provided on request, also kitchen and dining room where students can prepare own meals. Option of own or shared room. Non-smoking. Quiet, hardworking atmosphere. Weekly cleaning service provided.
B	Homestay—family with two children want student to live with them, share family meals, etc. Own room and access to family areas of house. International student preferred, so that children can learn about another culture.	F	3-bedroom house, one bedroom available. Three students in 20s share large comfortable living space, meals and housework. Want someone sociable who likes sharing meals, watching TV, listening to music, etc.
C	St Michael's College has vacancies for about 20 students. All-male college. All meals provided. Cleaning service included. First-year students share room, all others, own room.	G	Two-bedroom flat with one large double bedroom available. Owners are Mike and Sue—student and dentist—looking for single or couple to share. $150 a week. Non-smokers.
D	Single female looking for female flatmate. Vegetarian, relaxed approach. Share cooking and cleaning.	H	Small one-bedroom flat available for rent, $300 a week. Suit single or couple, no kids or pets. Access to communal garden and washing area.

KAPLAN)

8   Jenny, non-smoker, vegetarian. Looking to share a flat with just one other. Likes jazz and blues, walking and going to the beach.

9   Paul, 22-year-old engineering student, likes parties. Doesn't know how to cook and clean and doesn't want to learn! Only studies at exam time. Works in a gym part-time.

10 Ella, 20 years old, international student. Doesn't know anyone yet, would like to meet people. Wants accommodation where she can cook for herself. Has never shared housing with anyone except her parents.

11 Henry, 40-year-old mature student. Studying medicine, so has to study most of the time. Works part-time from home (on computer, consulting) and likes cooking in his free time. Budget: $100 a week. Smoker.

12 Cherie, 18, international student, first time away from home. Missing her family especially younger brothers and sisters. Doesn't know how to cook or clean, etc. Will go back to China for the holidays.

13 Robert, 23, Master's student. Sociable, has shared flats before, likes cooking. Goes out a lot. When home, likes to play video games and watch TV—and study.

14 Sally and Paul, young married couple from country town. Want own flat or share with another couple. Both study hard (vet science) and like to relax at home when not working—reading, dinner parties and music. Budget: $200 pw.

SECTION 2

You should spend about 20 minutes on **Questions 15 – 27**.

Questions 15 – 21

*Look at the information in the Service Guide for the University of Northwestern Australia below, and answer the questions using NO MORE THAN THREE WORDS. Write the answers in boxes **15-21** on your answer sheet.*

University of Northwestern Australia

SERVICE GUIDE

Here you will find a list of the full range of services offered to students at Northwestern. For further information, see our website at www.northwestern.co.edu.au

Health Services

Located on the Hartley campus there is a clinic available to all students. It is open only during term time (during holiday periods you must go to Casualty in town). To use the service, please ensure that you have both your student card and your Medicare card with you at all times. On presentation of these cards, treatment is free. There is a doctor and a nurse in attendance from 7 a.m. to 9 p.m. on weekdays, and from 7 a.m. to 12.30 p.m. on Saturdays. At all other times, please use the town hospital.

Transport

At first, Northwestern may feel a little isolated—especially if you are used to living in the centre of town. The site was chosen for its natural beauty and the peacefulness of the area is one of our most important assets. However, if you wish to enjoy the attractions of the local towns, don't despair—the public bus service is frequent and reliable, and additional university shuttle buses are available at peak times. To go to Thurile, catch the 45 bus from outside the Hartley main gates. It runs every 30 minutes on weekdays. If you wish to go to Gundini, catch the 67 bus from the Little campus—the stop is just near the football field. Both towns also have mini-cab services that offer competitive rates—so don't worry if you miss the buses once in a while!

Student Centre

The student centre is the "heart" of the university. Located on the Hartley campus, it comprises three buildings, and it is here that you will find a great variety of student services and leisure facilities. There is a career and job advisory service, where you can obtain advice regarding your chosen degree field; this service will also help you to find a part-time job.

KAPLAN

The two restaurants and three cafés in the student centre, as well as a reading room and games room, make it a comfortable home-from-home between classes. For those who wish to combine leisure with work, there is a computer centre for student use; additional computers are available in the library. And finally, the student centre is where the Students' Union have their offices and information boards. All students automatically become members of the Union when they pay their fees, so it's worth paying a visit to the union to find out more about what it can offer you.

International Student Office

Not to be confused with the student centre, this is where international students can go for information and advice regarding their academic or residential status. There is a team of academic experts here who can help with solutions to such problems as difficulties with English, or essay writing; they can also offer advice about future courses of study. There is also a lawyer available three days a week to help with visa and immigration solutions.

Shopping Information

Every item basic to a student's needs can be found here at the shops on the Hartley campus. There is a stationer's, which sells computer software as well as the usual pens, notebooks, etc.; and there is also a mini-market where you will find a wide range of food and drink, as well as cleaning products and basic medical supplies.

For other consumer needs, you may need to go into the nearest towns. Thurile has the biggest range of shops, most of them located on the main street. There you will find a supermarket, a boutique, an Asian food store and several good, reasonably-priced restaurants. Gundini, too, has a small supermarket, as well as a book store bookshop and video store. On Saturday mornings there is a wonderful farmers' market in Gundini, where you can find all sorts of fresh produce from the local farms and gardens.

15 Where should a student go to look for a part-time job opening?

16 Which bus would a student who wants to go to the bookshop take?

17 On which day can locally-grown vegetables be purchased?

18 Where should a student go for help renewing a visa?

19 Where can a student who gets sick on a Sunday go for medical help?

20 There is a computer room in the student centre. Where else can students find a computer to use?

21 If you wish to talk to a representative of the Students' Union, to which area should you go?

Questions 22-27

Read the course information for veterinary science below and complete the summary on page 210. Use NO MORE THAN THREE WORDS for each answer.

Course information and entry requirements for studying veterinary science at Northwestern Australia University

Course duration	5 years full-time
Units	96
Campus	Hartley
Course code	VTR101
Minimum education requirements, pre-requisites	Western Australia Year 12 or equivalent, English, mathematics, chemistry, physics. International students must also meet English language requirements (see International student website) and may be required to complete a foundation year at this or a related university.
Visa requirements	To be eligible for an Australian student visa, you must enrol in this programme full-time on campus at NWAU. A student visa requires a minimum attendance rate of 80%.
Fees	Enrolment fee of $220 (non-refundable). Total course cost $37,800.
Closing date	Applications must be lodged through the Western Australian Tertiary Admissions Centre. In order to commence study in Semester 1, 2009, the closing date for admission is September 30, 2008.
Enquiries	For further information, please call the admissions office at (61) 8 96873954, or see our website www.nwau.edu.au/int/enquiry.

Questions 22-27

Summary

If you wish to study veterinary science at Northwestern Australian University, you need to have completed schooling until Western Australia year 12 **22** ....…......... . You must have evidence of English language level proficiency (as outlined on the course website), and your school education must have included the following **23** ....…................. : English, maths, chemistry and physics. An Australian student visa is essential for this course of study—to be **24** ....…................ for a student visa you must enrol full-time for five years.

You must attend **25** ....…................ 80% of classes on a student visa.
The course costs $37,800, including a non-refundable admission fee of $220.

You must apply to the Western Australian Tertiary Admissions Centre **26** ....…................ September 30 if you wish to begin studying in Semester 1,

If you require **27** ....…................ , you can call or see the university website.

SECTION 3

You should spend about 20 minutes on **Questions 28 – 40**, which are based on Reading Passage 3 below.

Food for Thought

A Have you ever eaten a food that might kill you? That's what thousands of Japanese and Koreans do every year when they sit down to a delicious meal of *fugu* fish.

B *Fugu* is known in English as *puffer fish* and there are over 120 species of puffers in the World's oceans. They are relatively small, generally grey—sometimes with spots—and they have spikes, that pop up when they sense danger. Through these spikes they can inject a deadly venom into their attackers—and it is this venom which makes the fugu such a potentially dangerous dish.

C The venom is called tetrodotoxin and is mainly concentrated in the internal organs of the fish, though it is also found in the ovaries and the skin. Ingesting this poison causes damage to the nervous system, leading to symptoms ranging from numbness of the mouth to total paralysis. "The first sensation is numbness of the tongue and lips," says Dr Yuko Honda, a biologist at the Kansai Marine Institute. "This is soon followed by headache and dizziness, and often nausea and fatigue. The next symptom—and the most serious—is difficulty breathing, leading to paralysis."

D It is in Japan that *fugu* fish is most prized. Japanese law decrees that it must be prepared by a specially licensed fugu chef, who is legally bound to taste every dish before it is served. The chef is also required to dispose of the poisonous waste in a locked box. However, fugu is not as rare a dish as some people might think—in Tokyo alone it is served in some 3,000 restaurants; and it is also available at many supermarkets, sold in special trays with a security seal guaranteeing its safety.

E *Fugu* is usually eaten as sashimi, very thinly sliced and accompanied by rice and sake. It can also be eaten in *nabe* or hotpots—a kind of fish-soup—and even battered and fried. "*Fugu* is a fish with quite a delicate flavour," says Hiroshi Takamura, fugu chef at the popular Kintatsu restaurant in Tokyo, "so it's perfect for making sushi, which allows the flavour to be savoured. It needs to be cut very thinly, because it has quite firm flesh—I like to cut it so thin that the light shines right through it, though there are some chefs who cut it thicker." Asked about the dangers of eating fugu, Takamura becomes quite serious. "Obviously fugu must be prepared by a chef who knows how to do it," he says. "If the chef is licensed and careful, then there is no danger at all." And the poisonings we hear of sometimes? "That's when people buy the fish and try to prepare it themselves. Sometimes people are even sold fugu disguised as salmon or trout, which is a very dangerous practice."

F While the poison of fugu is known to be extremely toxic, there are still those who wish to try it. And why do people want to try such a dangerous toxin? Japanese food writer Naotaro Kageyama explains that it is "Because of the sensation they get on their lips and tongue from the poison. It's a kind of tingling numbness that is really quite strange… not unpleasant at all. This is one of the aspects of fugu that is most attractive to the true connoisseur."

G While there are those who wish to try the poison, every year there are many people sickened or killed by the poison accidentally. Kazuko Nishimura is one such victim. "Yes, I tried fugu just once. I didn't really want to, but my uncle had caught the fish and prepared it as a special treat, so we all sat down to a meal. At first, it was just my mouth, but then my head started to ache and then I couldn't breathe. They took me to hospital where I was in intensive care for a few days and they treated me for the poisoning, helping my body to breathe while I was paralysed." "Kazuko was very lucky to survive," says Doctor Harumi Matsui at the Kansai University hospital. "Fewer than 50% of victims of fugu poisoning survive, and it is not a very pleasant death. But Kazuko´s family brought her to the hospital immediately and we were able to keep her breathing while the poison wore off." Luckily no one else who shared the meal was affected—a single fugu has enough poison to kill up to 30 people, so the situation could have been much worse. It seems that Kazuko was the only one to eat a portion that contained the poison.

H If, after reading all this, you still wish to try fugu, you may have to travel a long way: Japan, Hong Kong, Korea, and the US are the only places that allow licensed chefs to prepare the dish. Fugu is completely illegal in Europe, and the rest of Asia and America. But if you can't travel that far to try it, you're in good company—the Emperor of Japan is not allowed to eat it either, forbidden by Royal decree.

Questions 28 – 32

Look at the following descriptions **(Questions 28 – 32)** *and the list of people below.*

Match each description with the correct person, **A, B, C, D** *or* **E.**

Write the correct letter, **A, B, C, D** *or* **E** *in boxes 28-32 on your answer sheet.*

28   *fugu* chef at Kintatsu

29   victim of *fugu* poisoning

30   biologist who studies *fugu*

31   doctor who treated *fugu* victims

32   food writer

List of People

    A   Yuko Honda

    B   Hiroshi Takamura

    C   Naotaro Kageyama

    D   Kazuko Nishimura

    E   Harumi Matsui

Questions 33 – 36

Do the following statements agree with the information in Reading Passage 3? In boxes
33-36 *on your answer sheet, write*

TRUE	*if the statement agrees with the information*
FALSE	*if the statement contradicts the information*
NOT GIVEN	*if there is no information on this*

33 A *fugu* chef must taste each dish before serving it to his customers.

34 More than 30 people die each year from *fugu* poisoning.

35 *Fugu* is popular because it has such a strong flavour.

36 The venom of the *fugu* is mainly concentrated in its skin.

Questions 37 – 38

Use the information given in the passage to answer **Questions 37-38** *below. Write the answers in boxes* **37-38** *on your answer sheet. Use ONLY ONE WORD for each space.*

37   What are the two types of places you can obtain *fugu* in Japan?

Restaurants and ....

38   In which four places are chefs licensed to prepare *fugu*?

Japan

Hong Kong

....

US

Questions 39 – 40

From the list of headings **1-7** *below, choose the most suitable heading for paragraph* **E** *and for paragraph* **G**. *Write the appropriate number in boxes* **39-40** *on your answer sheet*

1	Innocent Victims of the *Fugu*
2	Physical Reactions
3	Medical Treatment
4	Dishonest Fishermen
5	Many Ways to Eat *Fugu*
6	*Fugu* Chefs Are Well-trained
7	A Dangerous Practice

GENERAL TRAINING WRITING MODULE

WRITING TASK I

You should spend about 20 minutes on this task.

Last Tuesday you flew from New York to Paris. When you arrived home, you discovered that you had left your cabin bag on the plane.

Write a letter to the airline. In your letter, you should explain:

- **where and when you lost your bag**
- **what your bag looks like**
- **what its contents were**

Write at least 150 words.

You do NOT need to write any address. Begin your letter as follows:

Dear Sir or Madam:

WRITING TASK 2

You should spend about 40 minutes on this task.

Write about the following topic:

Some people are concerned that children spend too much time on computers—playing games, chatting and watching videos. But all this time is actually good preparation for children, who will have to spend many hours working on computers throughout their education and their working lives.

To what extent do you agree or disagree with this statement?

Give reasons for your answer and include any relevant examples from your own knowledge and experience.

Write at least 250 words.

KAPLAN

GENERAL TRAINING SPEAKING MODULE

TIME 10-15 minutes

PART ONE

Introduction to interview, 4-5 minutes

The examiner will begin by introducing him/herself and checking your identity.

S/he will then ask you some questions about yourself, based on everyday topics.

- Let's talk about the place where you live now.
- Describe the place where you live now.
- Were you born there?
- Do you live on your own or with your family?
- Has the place changed much over the time you have lived there? (How?)

PART TWO

Individual long turn, 3-4 minutes

Candidates' task card
INSTRUCTIONS

Please read the topic below carefully. You will be asked to talk about it for 1 to 2 minutes.

You will have one minute to think about what you're going to say.

You can make some notes to help you if you wish.

Describe a musical event you enjoyed attending.

You should say:

- **what the event you attended was**
- **where it took place**
- **who was with you**

and explain why you enjoyed attending the event.

The examiner may then ask you a couple of brief questions to show that this part of the test is over.

Further questions:

- Do you play music yourself?
- What instruments can you play?
- What kind of music do you most enjoy? What do you like about it?

PART THREE

Two-way discussion, 4-5 minutes

In Part Three the examiner will ask you further questions related to the topic in Part Two. Let's consider listening to music …

- How expensive is it to attend a concert in your country?
- Is it better to listen to live music, or to listen to music on the television or radio? Why is this better?
- Do you think there is too much music available now? Why/Why not?

Finally let's talk about famous musicians…

- Why do you think people are so interested in the personal lives of musicians?
- Is that interest stronger now than in the past?
- What are some of the things that can affect the image and popularity of musicians?

ANSWERS AND EXPLANATIONS

LISTENING MODULE (ACADEMIC AND GENERAL TRAINING)

Section I

1 (Greek)	Script – Latin and Greek
2 (Bengali)	Script – the Asian languages of Hindi and Bengali
3 (2)	Script – for two terms
4 (6994)	Script – sorry—6994
5 (Databases)	Script – February is going to be databases
6 (4)	Script – four slots left
7 (£60.00)	Script – It is £60.00 for the month
8 (June)	Script – No, on the third of June we start a Word course
9 (16)	Script – 16 vacancies
10 (6 p.m.)	Script – Please call her before 6 p.m.

Section 2

11 (University)	Script – the principal of Donleavy University
12 (3)	Script – which is one of the three campuses belonging to this University.
13 (office)	Script – This campus … is where I have my office
14 (ID passes)	Script – shown your ID passes to enter the site
15 (books and stationery)	Script – You can purchase all the required books and any stationery
16 (ID passes)	Script – you will still need to use them again to buy anything
17 ([memorial] fountain)	Script – a memorial fountain is being installed
18 (Physics)	Script – the office and administration block, is located between the Languages Centre, block 38, and the Physics School, block 30
19 (Shop)	Script – … it is between the Chemistry block … and the university shop, block 33
20 (Biology)	Script – The Biology block is block number 29, and you'll find block 29 between the Chemistry block and the Languages Centre

Section 3

21 (C)	Script – he diagnosed me with a migraine
22 (A)	Script – because we live near each other
23 (A)	Script – prepare a survey
24 (C)	Script – would you be willing to look up some references online?
25 (A)	Script – deodorants, cosmetics, soap
26 (B)	Script – people might think those things are a bit private
27 (B)	Script – I've made you a copy of my notes already, to save you time. Here you are!
28 (A)	Script – I'll catch up on the notes from last week
29 (C)	Script – I have to go to the library to collect some books
30 (C)	Script – Do you mean in the lab?

Section 4

31 (C)	Script – Being the curator
32 (B)	Script – an artist who has wide appeal
33 (B)	Script – Bright primary colours
34 (E)	Script – large canvases
35 (G)	Script – His paintings depicted birds, trees, flowers…
36 (bird)	Script – *Woman and Bird*
37 (park)	Script – It is on display in a park in Barcelona, often known as the Joan Miró Park
38 (mosaic)	Script – this sculpture is covered in mosaic
39 (1976)	Script – painted in 1976
40 (civil war)	Script – at a time when Miró was greatly influenced by events of the civil war in Spain.

KAPLAN

ACADEMIC READING MODULE

Reading Passage 1

1 (Not Given) — There is no information about the breakfasts eaten by mothers in India.

2 (Not Given) — There is no mention of new drugs in this article.

3 (True) — Text – Conventional wisdom states that the father's sperm is the main determinant of the child's gender. Paragraph 2.

4 (False) — Text – She changed the blood sugar level of female mice Paragraph 3.

5 (False) — Text – Although there was one study at the University of Exeter, England, Elissa Cameron's 2007 research was carried out at the African University of Pretoria. Paragraph 3.

6 (True) — Text – This could be ascribed to the decline in the number of adults and adolescent girls eating breakfast on a regular basis. Paragraph 6.

7 (Not Given) — There is nothing about tea in the article.

8 (False) — Text – High calorie diets have been shown to increase the likelihood of male births. Paragraph 7.

9 (A) — Text – She put an additive in the water to decrease the blood sugar levels. Paragraph 3.

10 (G) — Text – There are also health reasons... Paragraph 1.

11 (C) — Text – Her study followed 740 pregnant women who kept detailed records of their diets before conception. Paragraph 5.

12 (D) — Text – See the penultimate paragraph: This appears to make sense... from an evolutionary standpoint. Paragraph 7.

13 (K) — Text – Declining breakfast-eating habits could be biologically echoing the effects of scarcity, hence the decline in male births. Paragraph 6.

14 (C) — Text – If you would like to have a son, it might be a good idea to eat a breakfast that includes breakfast cereal. On the other hand, if you would prefer to give birth to a daughter, then cut out breakfast and continue a weight reduction diet at least until after conception. Paragraph 8.

Reading Passage 2

15 (B)   Text – MS patients can have one of two main varieties of the disease. Paragraph B.

16 (I)   Text – Sense of touch can be lost. Paragraph I.

17 (H)   Text – First, tiny patches of inflammation occur in the brain or spinal chord. Second, the protective coating around the axons, or nerve fibres, in the body starts to deteriorate. Third, the axons themselves become damaged or destroyed. Paragraph H.

18 (J)   Text – …no cure exists, although a number of medical treatments have been shown to reduce relapses and to slow the progression of the disease. Paragraph J.

19 (G)   Text – Where people live can be seen to have a clear effect. Paragraph G.

20 (Multiple Sclerosis)   Text – Multiple Sclerosis (MS) is a disease. Paragraph A.

21 (Relapse form)   Text – …the relapsing form and the primary progressive form. Paragraph B.

22 (10-15%)   Text – This condition affects about 10-15% of sufferers at diagnosis. Paragraph C.

23 (Where people live)   Text – Where people live can be seen to have a clear effect. Paragraph G.

24 (White/Caucasian)   Text – It commonly affects Caucasian people. Paragraph G.

25 (Colder)   Text – …and the incidence of MS is generally much higher in northern countries with temperate climates. Paragraph G.

26 (twin)   Text – …if one twin has the disease, then it is likely that the other twin will develop it. Paragraph F.

27 (spinal chord)   Text – First, tiny patches of inflammation occur in the brain or spinal chord. Paragraph H.

Reading Passage 3

28 (A) — Text – This steady electrical supply is subject to **minimal** variations. Paragraph 1.

29 (A) — Text – Most overcurrents are temporary and harmless. Paragraph 3.

30 (D) — Text – The most basic requirement of protective equipment is that it is *reliable* . Paragraph 5.

31 (B) — Text – …it is also advisable to purchase additional 'tripping' devices for sensitive electrical devices… Paragraph 8.

32 (D) — Text – …when the source of an overcurrent is far away, the overcurrent relays delay slightly before shutting down… Paragraph 7.

33 (A) — Text – …Each piece of equipment…must be protected by a *grounding* or *earthing* mechanism… Paragraph 6.

34 (True) — Text – …it should shut down the minimum number of devices. Paragraph 5.

35 (Not Given) — Text – No information is given about electricians.

36 (False) — Text – Electrical storms and lightning are among the biggest causes of major distribution overcurrent worldwide. Paragraph 4.

37 (True) — Text – …the grounding mechanism allows the excess electricity to be discharged into the earth. Paragraph 6.

38 (False) — Text – 67 people are killed every year by these types of storms. Paragraph 4.

39 (Not Given) — No information is given about this.

40 (False) — Text – …variations … are imperceptible to the consumer and do not normally harm electrical devices. Paragraph 2.

ACADEMIC WRITING MODULE

TASK I

This table describes global Internet use based on statistics from nine different countries in 2007. It includes three current parameters. The first is the number of Internet users for each country. The second is the percentage this comprises of the country's population. The third is the percentage of each country's Internet users in the world.

According to this table, the United States has the highest number of Internet users in the world, making up 18% of the world's users. However, Australia has the highest percentage of users in its population, with 71.9% of Australians online. Another country that has a high percentage of users is the United Kingdom, with 62.3% of its population using the Internet.

Although only 12.3% of China's population are Internet users, they make up 13.8% of world Internet users. Both Australia and the United Kingdom have a high percentage of Internet users. However, their mark on the world numbers is very small, under 3.5%. India, with 3.6% of the world's users is third in line after the US and China.

In conclusion, from the table it is clear that although Internet usage is prevalent worldwide, the percentage of users is low and hasn't even reached a quarter of the world's population.

(205 words)

TASK 2

In our world of media, advertisers are constantly searching for new and better ways to expose consumers to their products. The car industry has huge advertising budgets and tries to combine a variety of advertising venues in order to expose the highest number of consumers to their messages. The most popular car advertising is on television, billboards and in newspapers.

The advantage of advertising in newspapers is that car advertisers generally have an idea of the paper's readers and might have access to reader profiles. This could help them decide on the type of advertising to publish and help them create a highly focused campaign. However, newspapers also have a great disadvantage, with their short-term life span. Most expensive newspaper advertising usually ends up in the rubbish bin.

Billboards provide an effective place for car advertisers, especially along busy motorways, where drivers have a chance to daydream about the cars they wish they could afford. Strategically placed billboards can accomplish a high degree of exposure for car advertisers. Unfortunately, they don't leave a great deal of room for powerful messages. They can be passed up with a blink of the eye or a hoot from the driver behind you.

Television, unlike billboards and newspapers, enables advertisers to create more powerful and long-lasting messages. Car advertisers can highlight the most impressive features of their cars and target their potential markets at the same time. This dynamic medium offers minutes of air time during all hours of the day and night. Using the right market research, car advertisers can target viewers and strategically place their short film clips exactly at the time they know it will be most highly viewed by the right people. Yet, there are no guarantees. The greatest disadvantage for car advertisers is the fact that viewers tend to skip over commercials, opting to change channels when advertisements are aired.

In conclusion, car advertisers face real challenges when it comes to creating effective advertising campaigns that provide them with maximum exposure. In my opinion, television offers them the best way to meet these challenges. After all, television reaches the masses worldwide.

(352 words)

GENERAL TRAINING READING MODULE

Section 1, Questions 1 – 14

1 (132)   This is the cafeteria.

2 (212)   This is the waiting room for the Tropical Diseases Unit, where Dr Kynaston works.

3 (101)   This is the reception room of the Emergency Services Department.

4 (221)   This is the reception room of the Heart Disease Unit.

5 (133)   This is the Children's Playroom.

6 (122)   This is the reception room of the General Practice Unit; the text says to report to the reception area.

7 (Drink water)   Water is provided in coolers. The rules ask visitors not to eat or drink (except the water provided) and not to use their phones.

8 (D)   is the best answer because D is looking for a female flatmate and 8 only wants to share with one other person. Both are vegetarians.

9 (C)   is the best answer because in the College, 9 will not have to cook or clean, and will have the company of other students.

10 (E)   is the best answer, as in the Hostel, 10 will be meeting other students but not flat-sharing, which she has no experience of and may find difficult.

11 (A)   is the best answer because 11 needs accommodation where he can work hard; he can't afford the other two options where this would be possible (G and H).

12 (B)   is the best answer because 12 will be living with a family which will help her, as she is missing her own; and because she does not know how to cook or clean.

13 (F)   is the best answer because 13 has experienced flat-sharing and is sociable (the only other possibility is G—but that is needed for question 14).

14 (G)   is the best answer because the only other flat which meets their requirements is too expensive.

KAPLAN

Section 2, Questions 15 – 27

15 (Student Centre) ✓

The section of the text states that 'this service will also help you find a part-time job.'

16 (67) ✓

The section entitled *Shopping Information* tells us that 'Gundini has a bookshop', and the section entitled *Transport* says to catch the 67 bus to Gundini.

17 (Saturday) ✓

The section entitled *Shopping Information* states that 'on Saturday mornings there is a wonderful farmers' market in Gundini....'

18 (International Student Office) ✓

This section of the text states that 'There is also a lawyer available to help with visa and immigration solutions.'

19 (Town Hospital/Casualty) ✓

The section entitled *Health Services* states that University Health Services are available only on weekdays and Saturday mornings; 'At all other times, please use the town hospital.' This paragraph also states that 'during holiday periods you must go to Casualty in town', so this is another possible answer.

20 (The library/Library/ In the library) ✓

In the second paragraph of the section entitled *Student Centre*, the text states that 'additional computers are available in the library'.

21 (The Student Centre/ Student Centre) ✓

In the last two sentences of this section of the text, the Union is mentioned.

22 (or equivalent) ✓

From the beginning of the section entitled *Minimum education requirements/pre-requisites*.

23 (subjects) +

The information is contained in the section entitled *Minimum education requirements/pre-requisites* (the word itself is not used).

24 (eligible) ✓

From the section entitled *Visa requirements*.

25 (a minimum of) +

From the section entitled *Visa requirements*.

26 (before) ✓

From the section entitled *Closing date*.

27 (further information) +

From the section entitled *Enquiries*.

Section 3, Questions 28 – 40

28 **(B)**　　　　　　　from Paragraph E, lines 3 and 4.

29 **(D)**　　　　　　　from Paragraph G, lines 2-14.

30 **(A)**　　　　　　　from Paragraph C, lines 4-7.

31 **(E)**　　　　　　　from Paragraph G, line 8.

32 **(C)**　　　　　　　from Paragraph F, lines 2 and 3.

33 **(True)**　　　　　　from Paragraph D, line 2.

34 **(Not Given)**　　　No information is given about the number of deaths each year. In Paragraph G, the text states that one fish 'has enough poison to kill 30 people', to describe the potential strength of the poison.

35 **(False)**　　　　　Paragraph E, line 3 states that *fugu* has a delicate flavour.

36 **(False)**　　　　　Paragraph C, lines 1 and 2 state that the venom is 'mainly concentrated in the internal organs of the fish'.

37 **(Supermarkets)**　from Paragraph D, line 5.

38 **(Korea)**　　　　　from Paragraph H, line 2.

39 **(6)**　　　　　　　is the best answer for Paragraph E. While this paragraph also discusses different ways to eat fugu, the main topic is chefs and their training.

40 **(1)**　　　　　　　is the best answer for Paragraph G. The main topic of the paragraph is Kazuo Nishimura, an innocent victim. Although her symptoms are discussed, this is only a minor part of the paragraph.

GENERAL TRAINING WRITING MODULE

TASK I

Dear Sir or Madam,

I would like to report lost property. It seems that I left my red cabin bag on one of your flights. Last Tuesday, January 13th, I flew from New York to Paris on BA246 and took my red cabin bag with me. I put it in the overhead bin. Unfortunately, after the long flight, I must have forgotten it on the plane.

It's a red cabin bag on wheels. It has two outside pockets and is locked with a small lock. I had all of my school work and books in it. I also had a new sweater in it. I had just received it as a gift from my cousin in New York.

As you can imagine, these items are very important to me. Please let me know if you have my cabin bag and how I can get it back. Write to me at my return address or email: justinem@newcom.net

I'm looking forward to your reply.

Many thanks,

Justine Manfield

(164 words)

TASK 2

The world is online. Everyone is using computers for business and pleasure. There is growing concern about the effects this has on children. They spend many hours on the computer playing games, chatting and watching videos. Valuable childhood hours are spent sitting indoors opposite a computer screen instead of playing outdoors and running free.

Many people argue that the time children spend online is actually very good for them. They say that children have to prepare themselves for their higher education and working lives. Therefore, the time they spend is actually helping them gain the computer skills they need in order to become productive adults.

In my opinion, there are advantages and disadvantages to children spending a lot of time using computers. It is clear that children need computer skills to further their education. However, there is a difference between time spent playing computer games and chatting and the time spent working on school projects or doing online research. It is important to recognize that the online world is huge and offers limitless opportunities that are both useful and harmful.

Parents play a very important role in supervising the online activities of their children. It is their job to check the sites they are visiting and the games they are playing. It is also their duty to limit the number of hours that children spend in front of the computer. There are so many wonderful activities for children that don't involve the computer. Parents have to make sure that their children have a variety of interests outside the computer world.

In conclusion, it is clear that children today must be computer literate in order to succeed in life. But we have to remember that children should also experience many other joys of life that make childhood so special. It's possible to balance this out and make sure that children gain important computer skills and still enjoy the pleasures of childhood.

(320 words)

SPEAKING MODULE (ACADEMIC AND GENERAL TRAINING)

Part 1

Examiner: Hello , my name is …. Can you tell me your name, please?

Candidate: My name is ….

Examiner: Can you show me your I.D., please? Thank you.

Examiner: First, I'd like to ask you a few general questions about yourself. Where do you live?

Candidate: I live in Charlestown. It is a small city southeast from here, about a 30-minute drive away.

Examiner: Were you born there?

Candidate: No. I was born in Nagpur, a large city in India. It is in the western part of the country, near Mumbai.

Examiner: Do you live on your own or with your family?

Candidate: I live with two roommates. They are friends of mine from college. I have a sister who lives in Sydney, but the rest of my family still lives in Nagpur.

Examiner: How often to you get to see your family?

Candidate: Not very often. My parents visited me last year and I was in Australia two years ago on a student exchange, so I was lucky enough to see my sister as well.

Examiner: What are you studying?

Candidate: I started out studying to be a dentist and just hated it. I did it so that my parents would be happy. But then went for my true love, MUSIC!

Examiner: Oh, how long have you been studying music?

Candidate: I've been studying Hindu and Thai music for the last year and hope to graduate in two years time.

Examiner: Sounds great. Gook luck to you and thank you!

Part 2

Examiner: Now in this part, you need to talk about a topic for one minute. You can take a minute to make some notes before you speak. Here is a pencil and some paper for you, and the topic card. I would like you to talk about a musical event you have enjoyed attending.

(Candidate makes notes)

Examiner: Now, you have one minute to talk about the topic. I will tell you when to stop.

Candidate: A musical event I enjoyed attending was an opera. It was a presentation of La Boheme that took place at the Sydney Opera House. There were many reasons I enjoyed the event. First of all, I went there when I was doing my student exchange project and got a chance to see my sister Jane and meet some of her friends. We went with her friends Edward and Asha. Jane has been friends with them since she arrived in Sydney and started studying in college. It was great fun going to a new place with people I felt comfortable with. So it started off as a very pleasant experience.

The second reason I enjoyed it was that they knew so much about the opera house building. They couldn't stop talking about the famous Danish architect, Jorn Utzon, who built the building. I must admit it was all new to me.

The other reason I enjoyed the event is not only because of the music, but because of the building itself. It's located in a beautiful place, standing in harmony with the harbor. It has those unbelievable round roofs that look like waves. The best part of the building is the acoustics. It's unbelievable. You know I'm a musician and acoustics are very important to me.

I shouldn't forget the opera itself. I enjoyed it so much. I'm ashamed to say that it was the first time I had ever been to an opera. It was a very special moment for me to watch an opera on the stage for the first time. I have a feeling it's not going to be my last one.

Examiner: Do you play music yourself?

Candidate: Guitar and some other unusual instruments.

Examiner: What kind of music do you most enjoy? What do you like about it?

Candidate: I actually like oriental and rock music as well... My favorite bands are U2 and Coldplay. I like the guitar and the drums very much. I wish I could sing, too, but I don't have a very good singing voice!

Part 3

Examiner: Now in this part, I would like to ask you a few more general questions about the topic you've talked about. Since you're studying Hindu music, can you tell me a bit more about it? What is special about it?

Candidate: Oh, there are different kinds of Hindu music and they are very different from each other. For example there is folk and popular music and there is also classical music called Carnatic.

Examiner: What is Carnatic music?

Candidate: Oh, it's old Hindu music. It's more of a religious kind of music that most Indians like to listen to in the southern part of India. You know that India has different languages, and cultures, but this music is loved by all Indians. It is part of our history. It's very melodic and is based on singing more than on instruments.

Examiner: So what is so special about Hindu Music?

Candidate: Well, I think the first special thing about it is the musical instruments we play. There is the sitar, which everybody has heard about but there is another very popular instrument called sarod.

Examiner: What is that?

Candidate: Like the sitar, it's made of wood but it's covered with goat skin and has a very soft sound. You can even use it as a drum.

Examiner: Let's talk about modern music. What is happening in the world of rock and heavy metal?

Candidate:	There used to be very little rock music in India, but it has been developing. It actually started in the 70s when The Beatles visited India. Since there are lots of Indian rock bands and some of them have become famous all over the world. As of now, rock music in India is quietly growing day by day and getting a lot of support from the world. I think that what really helped was MTV which started in the early 1990s. This is when Indians began hear different kinds of rock and metal music. This music is popular in the big cities like Delhi and Mumbai.
Examiner:	And what are your plans after you graduate from college?
Candidate:	My dream is to finish studying here and then move back home and start my own band.
Examiner:	I wish you lots of luck. Thank you! That is the end of the test.

IELTS

PART 4:

AUDIO TRANSCRIPTS

AUDIO CD TRANSCRIPTS

In this section you will find the transcripts for the practice sections and the practice tests in the book.

How to Use These Transcripts

For Studying in General

It is recommended that you look at the transcripts after you do the listening exercises and fill in the answers in the book. Once you have checked your answers, you can listen to the exercise or section of the practice test again and try to answer the questions you have missed or did not understand. If you still cannot answer all the questions, look at the transcript in the section that corresponds to the listening section you are working on and read it to find the answer.

It is a good idea to look up the words you do not know in the dictionary to check their meaning and then listen to the recording again.

The words in **bold** in the answer key are the words that are important for understanding what the speaker says. They are almost always emphasised. You should listen for the words that the speaker pronounces with more emphasis. It is a good idea to underline these when listening to the recordings again.

You should also pay attention to the way the speakers connect the words they say. You can link the words in the sentences you do not understand well in the transcript to focus on pronunciation features. You can highlight the sentence stress and links in the sentence like this:

For When You Do Not / Cannot Use the CD

If you do not have the CD or cannot use it, you can use the transcripts to practise your reading. Here are some suggestions:

- If you have a friend or friends who can read English, ask them to read the transcripts aloud for you while you do the practice section or practice test.
- Record yourself or friends reading the transcripts.
- You can read them and answer the questions in the book.

KAPLAN

LISTENING PRACTICE SECTION 1

Narrator:	Listening Practice Section 1
Narrator:	You will hear a conversation between an IELTS candidate and an IELTS administrator. Look at the questions 1 – 5.
(30-sec. pause)	
Narrator:	Listen to the first part of the conversation and answer questions 1 – 5.
Candidate:	Good afternoon. I'm applying for a Master's programme at the University of Exeter in the UK. I'm planning to register for the IELTS exam at your centre next month. I have some questions I'd like to ask you before I register, if that's OK.
Administrator:	Certainly. Would you be taking the Academic Module?
Candidate:	I think so, but I'll have to contact the university just to make sure.
Administrator:	You'll probably need the Academic, because most universities don't accept the General Training ... And anyway, the procedures to register for the exam are the same for both the General and the Academic modules.
Candidate:	Good. My first question is whether I sit all parts of the exam on the same day. I don't live here, you see, and for me it would be more convenient to do all the papers on the same day.
Administrator:	Hmm. Unfortunately, the Speaking part is scheduled for Thursdays, and Reading, Writing and Listening tests take place on Saturdays. We can't change the days, I'm afraid.
Candidate:	Hmm. That's a pity. Well, never mind. What sort of documents do I need to bring in order to register?
Administrator:	You'll have to fill in the IELTS application form and bring an ID, a copy of your ID and two passport-size photos on a white background.
Candidate:	Will any ID do?
Administrator:	We only accept original passports and national IDs.
Candidate:	That's good to know. Did you say that Reading, Writing and Listening are scheduled for Saturdays?
Administrator:	That's right.
Candidate:	Will I get a break in between the papers?
Administrator:	I'm afraid there aren't any breaks between the papers. Each paper takes an hour to complete, so it's three hours straight through. You'll first do Listening, and then Reading followed by the Writing test. This is a standard requirement from Cambridge.

Narrator: Now look at the questions 6 – 10.

(30-sec. pause)

Narrator: As the conversation continues, complete questions 6 – 10.

Candidate: OK, and how soon after the test can I pick up my results?

Administrator: It takes 13 calendar days for the results to be processed.

Candidate: Can you let me know how much it is and the form of payment?

Administrator: The examination fee is US$200. You can pay by credit or debit card; we also accept cheques. We only accept cash as a form of payment in exceptional circumstances.

Candidate: And one last question. Can I mail you the application documents?

Administrator: Certainly. You can send all the documents by registered mail to our address: 47 Clover Place, New Rochelle, New York.

Candidate: Could you spell 'New Rochelle' for me, please?

Administrator: Certainly. N-E-W-R-O-C-H-E-L-L-E.

Candidate: Could I have the zip code as well?

Administrator: Sure, our zip code is 10806.

Candidate: Thanks.

Administrator: You can also e-mail us at inquiry@examsmail.com or phone us at 325-9082.

Candidate: I think that's all. Thank you very much for the information. Bye.

Administrator: You're welcome. Good-bye.

LISTENING PRACTICE SECTION 2

Narrator:	Listening Practice Section 2
Narrator:	You are going to listen to two students talking about a presentation on time management. Look at the questions 1 and 2.
(30 sec. pause)	
Narrator:	Now listen to the first part of the conversation and answer questions 1 and 2.
Lucy:	Hi, Mark. What're you doing?
Mark:	Hi, Lucy. Well, I'm preparing this seminar on time management. I'm supposed to do a presentation on the topic next week. Ironic, isn't it? I'm probably the worst student when it comes to time management.
Lucy:	I don't think you're that bad compared to some other people I know. Do you need some help with it?
Mark:	Yeah, I just don't know where to start, to be honest.
Lucy:	When are you doing the presentation?
Mark:	I'm supposed to hand in the draft on Wednesday at 11.00 a.m. The presentation is scheduled for 10.00 a.m. this Friday.
Narrator:	Now look at the questions 3 – 10.
(30-sec. pause)	
Narrator:	As the conversation continues, complete questions 3 – 10.
Lucy:	That's not too bad. This gives you the whole weekend to prepare. Let's brainstorm some ideas, shall we? Do you want to get pen and paper to jot down some thoughts? I think you should start with a broad, general statement, for example: 'I read somewhere that organising time is a skill like learning to drive or tying your shoelaces.' Then you could move onto discussing the common problems people have with managing time.
Mark:	That's not a bad idea. One of the common problems is putting things off.
Lucy:	Yeah, you could also mention some common signs of this symptom, such as last-minute holiday shopping, putting off visits to the doctor's or the dentist's. Another problem is relying too much on your memory and not writing things down.
Mark:	Do you mean not keeping a diary or a planner to plan the tasks?
Lucy:	That's right. For example, writing down what I need to do in a diary or a planner helps me remember what I need to do and makes me more focused on the tasks for the day.
Mark:	Good idea. That reminds me of something I've being meaning to do for a while now. Anyway, I should also include some advice on how to deal with the problem, shouldn't I?
Lucy:	Sure. You can talk about some ways of stopping procrastination.

Mark: I guess making a 'to do' list can help one focus on what needs to be done.

Lucy: Definitely. Another way to deal with the problem is to prioritise and do the hardest job first, the one which requires the most effort and concentration. Also, my tutor recommended that I should break big projects into small parts with a specific goal. Having an action plan has worked for me. I usually make a list of small tasks I need to do to achieve a goal. Sometimes I just don't feel like getting down to work because a task seems too overwhelming for me to even think about. This technique helps me reduce psychological pressure if I think of a project as a set of easily achievable tasks, don't you think?

Mark: I know what you mean. I often feel like that myself with the statistics project I've been doing this term. I'm well behind and the deadline is next week.

Lucy: I think setting deadlines and sticking to them can help one to achieve goals. You can discuss this aspect in your presentation, too.

Mark: A good point. Setting deadlines can also help one become more realistic about the time it takes to do tasks.

Lucy: Another point you could include is how to deal with interruptions.

Mark: OK. I guess blocking in time to handle unpredictable interruptions can help one stay focused.

Lucy: Not just that. Some interruptions such as phone calls can be easily avoided by using an answering machine, for example. Saying 'No', which is one of the most useful words in English, is also very effective. It can be tough sometimes, but you've got to learn to say it nicely but firmly. I think you've got enough ideas here to start with.

Mark: Definitely. Thanks a lot for your help. I just need to type the ideas up and I think I'm all set. Do you think you can lend me your laptop for a couple of hours?

Lucy: Mmm... I'm afraid I can't. I've got to finish my own project.

Mark: Never mind, I'll use one at the library. You certainly know how to say 'No'!

Lucy: Learnt it the hard way. Got to go now. Good luck with the presentation.

Mark: Cheers. See you later.

LISTENING PRACTICE SECTION 3

Narrator:	Listening Practice Section 3
Narrator:	You are going to listen to a radio programme on sleep deprivation. Look at the questions 1 – 5.

(30-sec. pause)

Narrator:	Now listen to the first part of the programme and answer questions 1 – 5.
Presenter:	With us in the studio today are Dr. Peter Collins, a senior lecturer in the Department of Psychology at the University of Chicago, and Helen Gardner, the author of the book *Deep Sleep*. They've come to our studio to discuss the effects of sleep deprivation and also give some tips to the sleep-deprived on how to deal with the problem. Welcome to the studio, Helen and Peter.
	Now Peter, what are the reasons for sleep deprivation, and how can it affect our lives?
Peter:	Well, the research into sleep deprivation started in the late 50s and has been going on ever since. Many researchers link sleep deprivation with electricity, television and computers, which have enabled humans to work 24/7. Before electricity was invented, people's body clocks were synchronised with the sun's schedule, and the average time they spent sleeping was eight to nine hours a night. By 1975, that average was down to seven hours, and today one-third of us sleep less than six hours a day.
	This leads to a condition called 'chronic sleep deprivation', which basically means going for extended periods of time with less sleep than your body needs. Chronic sleep deprivation can cause a variety of physical and psychological problems. At its most basic level, loss of sleep can make us more irritable and less efficient, and can affect long-term memory and concentration, which can result in more accidents.
	According to the latest research into sleep deprivation, sleep deprivation is the main reason for three per cent of plane crashes, ten per cent of domestic accidents, 20 per cent of accidents at work, and 45 per cent of all traffic accidents.
	Research into the physical effects of chronic sleep deprivation suggests more serious and significant long-term complications.
	Research from my university—the University of Chicago—has shown that sleep deprivation interferes with how the human body regulates insulin and sugar metabolism, which can increase the risk of diabetes.
	People who are sleep-deprived have weakened immune systems and are more prone to viruses and other kinds of infections.
	People who don't get enough sleep have cognitive problems or difficulties processing and assimilating new information. Lack of sleep affects long-term memory, and slows down such abilities as judgment and reaction times.
	Some researchers link sleep deprivation with obesity, indicating that sleep disorders and eating disorders are often linked.

Narrator: Now look at the questions 6 – 10.

(30-sec. pause)

Narrator: As the programme continues, answer questions 6 – 10.

Presenter: Helen, you've done a fair amount of research for your recent book on helping people deal with sleeping problems. Could you give our listeners some tips on managing their sleep?

Helen: Well, if you spend several hours a night tossing and turning in bed trying to fall asleep, you first have to find out how much sleep you need. To do so, you'll need to try and sleep six to nine hours a night. Set aside three days for the experiment. It's best to do it on a long weekend or a holiday to ensure it doesn't get interrupted.

During the experiment, you should go to bed at the same time every night and give yourself six, seven, eight or nine hours of sleep. Then monitor the way you feel throughout the day to find out how many hours of sleep you need in order to feel your best.

Once you find out how much sleep you need, you can work on improving the quality of your sleep.

The main secret here is to allow yourself one or two hours to relax before going to bed.

You may want to try and have a warm shower or bath before going to bed. Doing some quiet activities such as reading or filing can help some people relax. A warm drink in bed helps to induce sleepiness. Some people take up yoga or meditation to help them relax at night.

Different techniques will work for different people, so it's best to experiment and find the one that suits you best.

You should definitely avoid using technology before going to bed. Activities such as playing video games, watching TV and others which require you to use your attention can stop you from falling asleep.

Avoid eating before going to bed. A late dinner can disrupt your sleep. Not only is going to bed with a heavy stomach bad for digestion and can make you overweight, but it can also keep you awake for hours.

Caffeine-rich drinks can increase your heart rate, which can stop you from falling asleep. Energy drinks also have the same effect on your body. You should avoid drinking these at night.

The same goes for vigorous physical exercise such as weight-lifting or working out on a treadmill.

In many cases you can re-set your body clock and make it tick for you by changing your lifestyle.

If your sleep deprivation is severe, it's always best to seek professional advice and get an appointment with your doctor, who might prescribe you sleeping pills.

KAPLAN

Presenter: Thank you, Helen. We'll be back after the break and we'll be answering questions we've received from our listeners...

LISTENING PRACTICE SECTION 4

Narrator:	Listening Practice Section 4
Narrator:	You are going to listen to a lecture on language learning. Look at the questions 1 – 10.

(30-sec. pause)

Narrator:	Now listen to the lecture and answer questions 1 – 10.
Lecturer:	This is the first in our series of lectures on language learning. The topic I'd like to deal with today is: What makes a successful language learner?

There's been a lot of research into what makes some people learn a language faster than others. In this lecture, I'll summarise the main findings of the research into the subject.

There are many factors that influence how quickly one learns a foreign language, of which exposure to the target language seems to be one of the most important factors to consider. It's this factor which determines the speed of learning a language, especially among those people who learn a foreign language outside the classroom. There are more people who did not learn a second or a third language in the classroom, and I think that understanding how learners successfully learn languages without the help of a teacher can provide us with the key to how to become a successful language learner.

Let's look then at the characteristics of a successful language learner. Motivation seems to be one of the key factors. Research into motivation has identified two main types: instrumental motivation and integrative motivation.

Instrumental motivation is the kind of motivation that encourages people to learn a language for practical reasons such as getting a job or passing an examination. Learners with this kind of motivation intend to use the target language as a tool or instrument to help them achieve a goal.

Integrative motivation is what encourages learners to learn a language in order to communicate and socialise with others who speak the language. The primary aim for learners with integrative motivation is to use the language to integrate and identify with the community that uses the language. Immigrants or people who are married to speakers of another language are motivated in this way. Although most people have mixed motivation, research into language learning and acquisition suggests that integrative motivation produces much better results, and is an important characteristic of successful language learners.

Personality is another important factor in language learning. One does not need to be an extrovert to learn a foreign language, but willingness to experiment and take risks is essential. Introverted or anxious learners who are afraid of making mistakes find it harder to learn a language. Good language learners will try to experiment with different ways of learning vocabulary or grammar until they find the way that suits them best.

Language is a complex system. Successful language learners often design complex learning systems to master a language. They think about how they learn, and organise their learning accordingly. They develop their own learning style and use a range of learning skills such as efficient revision techniques, systems for learning and organising vocabulary, the ability to monitor their own speech and the ability to plan their learning.

Finally, age is another major factor to be borne in mind. Children seem to be in the best position to learn a foreign language rapidly and with the best results. Older learners can also be very successful and become proficient at using a language. Adult learners who make decisions about their learning and are independent of the teacher, who are analytical and aware of how they learn, and who take responsibility for their learning, stand a very good chance of learning a foreign language successfully.

LISTENING TEST TRANSCRIPTS

SECTION 1 (QUESTIONS 1 – 10)

Receptionist: Good morning, Clevedon College, can I help you?

Caller: Yes, please. I'd like some information about evening courses this term...

Receptionist: OK...which Which subjects are you interested in?

Caller: Two subjects, actually, Languages and Computer Skills.

Receptionist: OK. What languages are you interested in?

Caller: Actually, I'm not sure. I have to fulfil a language requirement for school, but I haven't really decided what language to study. Um...how many language courses do you run each week?

Receptionist: We have two every night, from Monday to Friday.

Caller: I'm sorry, but would you mind going through the schedule for me? Um... which languages on which days...?

Receptionist: Not at all. Monday to Wednesday are Modern European Languages: French, Spanish, German, Dutch and Polish. Thursday night we offer ancient languages, Latin and Ancient Greek. And on Friday we finish off with the Asian languages of Hindi and Bengali.

Caller: Monday to Wednesday, Modern European; Thursday, Ancient Languages, and Friday, Asian...Can you spell Bengali please?

Receptionist: Yes, it's B-E-N-G-A-L-I.

Caller: Great. And, how much do the courses cost?

Receptionist: Each course costs £25.00 per person per term, but if you want to do TWO language courses, there's a 10% discount, but only if you book for two terms.

Caller: So the 10% discount is if I take two courses, for two terms, is that right?

Receptionist: Right.

Caller: Would it be possible for me to book my classes right now?

Receptionist: No, sorry, the computer's down. What I suggest you do is call extension 9694 ...no, sorry...6994, after 6.00 p.m. and ask for Mrs Johnson.

Caller: I'm sorry, I didn't get that. Did you say 6994...after 6.00 p.m.?

Receptionist: Yes, 6994...please ask for Mrs Johnson.

Caller: Thanks. OK, can we now look at the Computer Skills Courses?

Receptionist: Yes, of course. Computer classes always start in the first week of the month, and the way it works is, we offer one computer class for the entire month. So you might spend one month on databases...another month on Excel, and so on. Classes meet once a week, on Tuesday afternoons. The next class starts February 1st.

Caller: OK, so for the upcoming month...February...?

Receptionist:	February is going to be Databases. There are 24 places still free on that course and it costs £40.00 per person.
Caller:	February...databases...24 openings...£40.00...OK...
Receptionist:	Excel starts in March and that's nearly full – only four slots left. It's £45.00.
Caller:	OK, Excel...March...only four slots left...got it.
Receptionist:	April is Outlook. That is never as popular since it costs so much more, but you get a free CD. It is £60.00 for the month, and there are 19 places left.
Caller:	OK, April...Outlook...£60.00...Is that it?
Receptionist:	No, on the third of June we start a Word course. We have 16 vacancies for that at the moment. It's also expensive at £55.00.
Caller:	Third of June...Word...16 vacancies...£55.00...Now, do I call the same number to book a place in one of these classes?
Receptionist:	No, you have to call Mary Jones, I think. Yes, Mary Jones...extension 9623.
Caller:	Sorry, could you repeat that number?
Receptionist:	Yes...extension 9623. Please call her before 6.00 p.m.
Caller:	OK. Many thanks for all your help.

Section 2 (Questions 11 – 20)

Good afternoon, ladies and gentlemen. I'm Dr. Donovan, the Principal of Donleavy University, and I would like to welcome you to the Dingle Wood Campus, which is one of the three campuses belonging to this University. This campus, Dingle Wood, is where I have my office, and it's also the location of the Languages and Science Campus, so some of you will be studying here. Dingle Wood is the most northerly campus. The Business Studies Blocks are in the Churchdown Campus in the centre of town, and the southern or Trailway campus, where History and Architecture are situated, is to the south of the town. Those of you who are enrolled in any of those courses will be taken to your respective buildings at the end of this meeting. Those of you studying in on the Dingle Wood campus...you will have a tour later, too.

This building we are assembled in is the office or administration block—block 39—and is where the weekly meetings are held. You are welcome to attend these meetings as are all the University staff. You may want to, as many university issues are discussed at these weekly meetings. The meetings take place at 1.30 every Tuesday, so please stop by. Two other important buildings are also located on this campus, the cafeteria and the on-site shop. You can purchase all the required books and any stationery you need for your courses at this shop. Please bear in mind that, even though you have shown your ID passes to enter the site, you still need to use them again to buy anything in the shop or cafeteria ...This is for security reasons.

[Speaker pauses briefly]

Now if I could draw your attention to the back page of your Joining Instructions booklet, you will see a small map of this campus—Dingle Wood. The block we are in now, the office and administration block, is located between the Languages Centre, block 38, and the Physics School, block 30, that's three-oh. These are both on the right of the plan. The cafeteria, which is open from 7.00 a.m. to 9.30 p.m., is on the left of the plan. It is between the Chemistry block, number 35, and the university shop, block 33. At the university shop you can get all you will need in terms of course materials.

The Biology block is block number 29, and you'll find the Biology block between the Chemistry block and the Languages Centre. Be careful with the numbers, as they are not always logical.

As you will see, there are gardens on the right hand side of the gate. These are being extended over the next two months and a memorial fountain is being installed in the middle of the campus. This means that the campus will be very noisy during normal working hours; however, the campus will look much nicer when it is all finished.

Right, so that's it for your initial campus orientation. At this point, could the language students all follow me, please, and the rest of you—please assemble under the banners which show your main topic of study and you will be directed to the other campuses.

SECTION 3 (QUESTIONS 21 – 30)

Sarah:	Hi Bill. How are you?
Bill:	I'm OK now, Sarah, but I was so ill last week.
Sarah:	Oh dear, what was the problem? Did you eat that dodgy fish in the canteen?
Bill:	No. At first I thought it was a cold, but then my head started hurting and my eyes started to go blurry...
Sarah:	I'm so sorry...that sounds serious...
Bill:	It's OK, actually. I went to the doctor and he diagnosed me with a migraine. He gave me some medicine, and I'm starting to feel much better.
Sarah:	I'm glad to hear that. Well, I'm also glad you're in today because we have to work on a new project together.
Bill:	Oh, are we in the same section?
Sarah:	No, it's just us—no one else. Mr Donaldson put us down as B team because we live near each other.
Bill:	That could be fun! What do we have to do?
Sarah:	Well, the project is partly Internet research, then checking reference books for information to prepare a survey, which we have to use with people we know.
Bill:	Great, what's the topic?
Sarah:	It's to do with shopping over the last 10 years. We have to find out how customers have changed their behaviour.
Bill:	OK...so, what's the first step?
Sarah:	I think the first thing to do is to check the list of references he gave me. But my computer is in for repair, so...if I check in the reference library, would you be willing to look up some references online? Once we're done with the reference checks, we can write the questions together.
Bill:	That's fine, I'll do the Internet research. So...what sort of shopping are we looking at? Only food, or goods, or clothes shopping...?
Sarah:	We have to find people who are willing to tell us about personal things like deodorants, cosmetics, soap or vitamin creams. The other groups are doing food, electrical goods and clothes.
Bill:	That won't be so easy, Sarah; people might think those things are a bit private.
Sarah:	Yes, I thought about that. I'll ask the women and you can ask the men. That should work OK.
Bill:	Well, if you think so...Give me the list of references then.
Sarah:	Sorry, I left them in my other bag at Joseph's house. I'll get them for you tomorrow.
Bill:	OK. Well, then, this afternoon I think I'll catch up on the notes from last week. Can you help me or are you busy?
Sarah:	I've made you a copy of my notes already, to save you time. Here you are!
Bill:	Wow, thanks, Sarah, that's so thoughtful! Well, since there's nothing for us to do right now, shall we go for lunch...?

Sarah:	Actually, I'll have to catch you later, I have to go to a meeting this afternoon. Can I phone you tonight to arrange when to meet?
Bill:	No, sorry, I have a date. Can we meet in the laboratory for the first class tomorrow?
Sarah:	I'm not sure because I have to go to the library to collect some books…What about meeting there at lunchtime?
Bill:	Do you mean in the lab?
Sarah:	Yes.
Bill:	OK, see you at in the laboratory tomorrow at noon, then. Sounds like we have a lot of work to do.

SECTION 4 (QUESTIONS 31 – 40)

Good evening, everybody, and welcome to the first in this year's series of public lectures offered by the Art Gallery. As chief curator of the gallery, I was given the honour of presenting the first lecture—and, let me tell you, I had a difficult time deciding what to talk about tonight.

Being the curator, I naturally know just about everything that's in this gallery, but I wanted to choose an artist who has a wide appeal—that seems only fair, yes? But I didn't want to talk about someone so well-known that anything I said would be familiar. I wanted someone modern—my personal preference is for modern art—but again, I wanted to choose someone who had the potential to appeal to all art lovers, whether they're attracted to traditional forms, Impressionism, Surrealism, or what have you.

So, having spent the last five years as a visiting professor in Barcelona, it's not surprising that I finally chose to talk about one of the greatest Catalan artists—one whose work is likely to be familiar to many of you: Joan Miró.

Look at this...and this...and this. Ring any bells?! Miró's most famous—and most widely-reproduced—works tend to be like this. Bright primary colours, with lots of asymmetrical forms. He painted on large canvases—larger than himself, quite often—and his paintings depicted birds, trees, flowers and other features of the natural world. But Miró produced a great variety of work, and it's about some of his lesser-known paintings that I would like to speak this evening.

Miró was born in Barcelona in 1893, the son of a goldsmith. He began to show talent very early, and in 1926, went to Paris where he was drawn to the Surrealists of Montparnasse. He did not define himself as a Surrealist, however; he preferred to stay free to experiment with other artistic styles as he wished. Miró had an intense dislike of much of the painting and many of the painters he knew. He wished to do something totally different, to express his contempt for bourgeois art—and yet, ironically, Miró's success has made his works much in demand among art collectors of the world.

But we can't really talk about the artist without looking at his art, and that's what I'd like to do now—to take a look at just a few of Miró's works and think about what it is that makes them special—special to me, and to a great number of people who flock every day to the Miró Foundation in Barcelona.

Let's start with this, one of Miró's best-known and brightest works—*Woman and Bird*, a sculpture created in 1982. It is on display in a park in Barcelona, often known as the Joan Miró Park. A huge sculpture, towering up into the sky, it reflects Miró's eternal interest in these themes, as well as his more technical interest in materials; this sculpture is covered in mosaic, which gives it a naïve and cheerful appearance. It is interesting that this sculpture was completed in 1982, just a year before Miró's death. I think it shows that, towards the end, he was feeling as playful as a young man, and I think he wanted to share this playfulness in a park, on such a big, very public scale.

And now, another representation of a woman, this time, just called *Woman*. This was painted in 1976—a late work for Miró—and is a work we often see reproduced, or on sale as postcards or posters in gallery shops around the world. So why is it so popular? I think the use of colour has something to do with it; people respond to these rounded shapes filled with primary colours, especially on a large canvas like this. Also the fact that, while it is rather surreal, it is still possible to recognise the form of a woman, and to see it as a sympathetic representation. It's a bold, bright painting, and I think that it awakens a reaction in many of us.

And finally, something quite different—though still a woman. A harsh, even violent work that was completed in 1939, at a time when Miró was greatly influenced by events of the civil war in Spain. It's titled *Seated Woman II*, but it can be hard to find the woman here, as she's been transformed into rather a horrendous creature. So is that how Miró viewed women—as grotesque? Not at all. This picture can also be seen as strong, with a huge base and solid shoulders to support those who depend on her. In this painting, her arms and neck seem to grow as vegetation out of her shoulders—representing woman as a fertile ground, perhaps. We also see here the fish and birds, the moon and stars so typical of Miró's work—making her a creature of nature and of the heavens as well.

And that's all we have time for this evening, I'm afraid. I hope that you've enjoyed this brief look at Miró's work, and that you will enjoy the other lectures that follow this one.

Thank you and good night.

NOTES

NOTES

NOTES

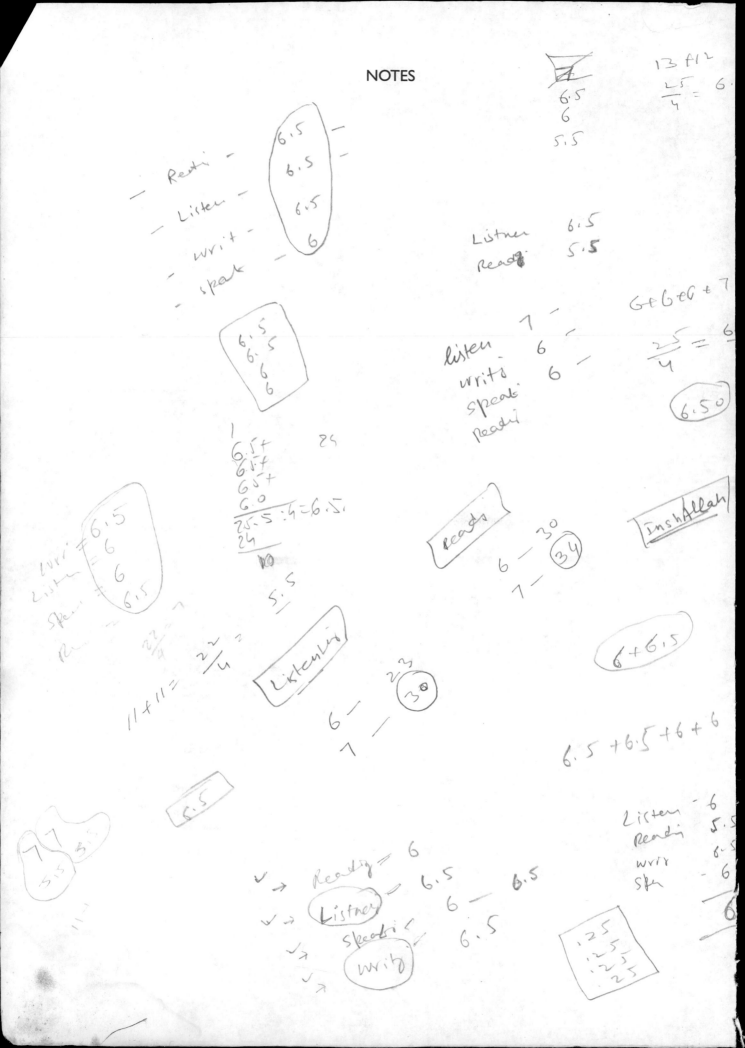

NOTES

SOFTWARE LICENSE/DISCLAIMER OF WARRANTIES

1. ACCEPTANCE. By using this compact disc you hereby accept the terms and provisions of this license and agree to be bound hereby.

2. OWNERSHIP. The software contained on this compact disc, all content, related documentation and fonts (collectively, the "Software") are all proprietary copyrighted materials owned by Kaplan, Inc. ("Kaplan") or its licensors.

3. LICENSE. You are granted a limited license to use the Software. This License allows you to use the Software on a single computer only. You may not copy, distribute, modify, network, rent, lease, loan or create derivative works based upon the Software in whole or in part. The Software is intended for personal usage only. Your rights to use the Software and this License shall terminate immediately without notice upon your failure to comply with any of the terms hereof.

4. ADDITIONAL RESTRICTIONS. The Software contains copyrighted material, trade secrets, and other proprietary material. In order to protect them, and except as permitted by applicable legislation, you may not decompile, reverse engineer, disassemble or otherwise reduce the Software to human-perceivable form.

5. LIMITED WARRANTY; DISCLAIMER. Kaplan warrants the compact disc on which the Software is recorded to be free from defects in materials and workmanship under normal use for a period of ninety (90) days from the date of purchase as evidenced by a copy of the receipt. Kaplan's entire liability and your exclusive remedy will be replacement of the diskette or compact disc not meeting this warranty. The Software is provided "AS IS" and without warranty of any kind, and Kaplan and Kaplan's licensors EXPRESSLY DISCLAIM ALL WARRANTIES, EXPRESS OR IMPLIED, INCLUDING THE IMPLIED WARRANTIES OF MERCHANTABILITY OR FITNESS FOR A PARTICULAR PURPOSE. FURTHERMORE, KAPLAN DOES NOT WARRANT THAT THE FUNCTIONS CONTAINED IN THE SOFTWARE WILL MEET YOUR REQUIREMENTS, OR THAT THE OPERATION OF THE SOFTWARE WILL BE UNINTERRUPTED OR ERROR-FREE, OR THAT DEFECTS IN THE SOFTWARE WILL BE CORRECTED. KAPLAN DOES NOT WARRANT OR MAKE ANY REPRESENTATIONS REGARDING THE USE OR THE RESULTS OF THE USE OF THE SOFTWARE IN TERMS OF THEIR CORRECTNESS, ACCURACY, RELIABILITY OR OTHERWISE. UNDER NO CIRCUMSTANCES, INCLUDING NEGLIGENCE, SHALL KAPLAN BE LIABLE FOR ANY DIRECT, INDIRECT, PUNITIVE, INCIDENTAL, SPECIAL OR CONSEQUENTIAL DAMAGES, INCLUDING, BUT NOT LIMITED TO, LOST PROFITS OR WAGES, IN CONNECTION WITH THE SOFTWARE EVEN IF KAPLAN HAS BEEN ADVISED OF THE POSSIBILITY OF SUCH DAMAGES. CERTAIN LIMITATIONS HEREIN PROVIDED MAY BE PRECLUDED BY LAW.

6. EXPORT LAW ASSURANCES. You agree and certify that you will not export the Software outside of the United States except as authorized and as permitted by the laws and regulations of the United States. If the Software has been rightfully obtained by you outside of the United States, you agree that you will not re-export the Software except as permitted by the laws and regulations of the United States and the laws and regulations of the jurisdiction in which you obtained the Software.

7. MISCELLANEOUS. This license represents the entire understanding of the parties, may only be modified in writing and shall be governed by the laws of the State of New York.